ALONE AND ON FOOT

Alone and on Foot

Ignatius of Loyola

BRIAN GROGAN SJ

VERITAS

First published 2008 by
Veritas Publications
7/8 Lower Abbey Street
Dublin 1
Ireland
Email publications@veritas.ie
Website www.veritas.ie

ISBN 978 1 84730 134 5

10 9 8 7 6 5 4 3 2 1

Designed by Vivienne Adu-Boahen
Cover design by Vivienne Adu-Boahen, based on the sculpture of
Ignatius the Pilgrim by Bill McElcheran
Printed in the Republic of Ireland by ColourBooks Ltd, Dublin

Veritas books are printed on paper made from the wood pulp of managed
forests. For every tree felled, at least one tree is planted, thereby renewing
natural resources.

Contents

Acknowledgements

Thanks to J. Ignacio Tellechea Idigoras, 1928–2008, Spain's premier Renaissance historian, who wrote his biography of Ignatius as a labour of love. Titled *Ignacio de Loyola: solo y a pie*, it was published in 1987.

Thanks to Loyola Press, Chicago, for graciously permitting the publication of this abridgement of *Ignatius of Loyola, The Pilgrim Saint* by Jose Ignacio Tellechea Idigoras, translated by Cornelius M. Buckley SJ (Loyola Press, 1994). To order copies of this book, contact Columba Bookservice at + 353 1 294 2556 or visit *www.columba.ie*

Thanks to the staff of Veritas Publications for their encouragement and professional expertise, and to John White of the Jesuit Communications Centre, Dublin, who augmented the illustrations, of which six originally appeared in *Autobiografia de San Ignacio*, published by the Jesuits of Paraguay in 1991, and which are used with their permission.

Lastly, thanks to my Jesuit and other friends, female and male, from whom I have learnt so much as we travelled together the road of Ignatian spirituality. I am grateful for their ongoing support and encouragement when this project got bogged down, and especially when it literally went up in flames on Good Friday 2007.

Brian Grogan SJ
15 August 2008
(Feast of the Assumption of Our Lady)

Introduction

Most people today would be hard pressed if interviewed about Ignatius of Loyola, 1491–1556. Perhaps a few might volunteer the following: 'Wasn't he injured by a cannonball?'; 'During his convalescence, didn't he get an insight that changed his life?'; 'I think he founded the Jesuits way back'. Even the countless numbers who today shape their lives by Ignatian spirituality often feel that they know little about Ignatius himself. In contrast to his companion St Francis Xavier, he is an obscure and complex figure, and historians have fastened on diverse aspects of his life, often to the exclusion of others that could reveal a more holistic picture of the man.

The Cambridge Companion to The Jesuits, 2008, sketches five dimensions of Ignatius, and one could add more. He is 'the pilgrim' who can be understood only in his intimate relationship with God, who guided him both on earthy and on mystical paths. He is the caring and compassionate figure whose primary concern, as he says himself, is 'to help others', a dimension of his life that is often missed. He is most frequently portrayed as the superior of the companions he had gathered over the years, deploying them across the world. He is the loyal servant of a troubled Church and the wise author of the Spiritual Exercises, of the Constitutions, and of more than seven thousand letters. He is cast as the leader of the Counter-Reformation, but wrongly, because Protestantism was only a peripheral concern for the early Jesuits. Likewise he is caricatured as harsh and dictatorial, whereas in fact he had a highly attractive personality and referred to his companions as 'friends in the Lord'. It is not surprising that a study of Ignatius by Irish Jesuit Joe Veale in 2001 bore the title: 'Are You Sure You Know Who I am?'

How did Ignatius come to have such an extraordinary influence on the world of his time? Why, five hundred years on, is this influence greater than ever? Why have there been some five thousand editions of his Spiritual Exercises since the first publication in 1548 – more editions than there are months between then and now? Why are the Exercises included among the books that have changed the world?

The explanation, as we shall see further on, is that Ignatian spirituality can enable you to do what Ignatius did in his day, that is, to make sense of your life experiences and to interpret them in the light of God's dreams for yourself. Ignatian spirituality was crafted painstakingly by a sixteenth-century

Basque struggling alone to make sense of his disjointed and seemingly pointless life, in a world as chaotic and fragmented as our own. Only when wounded in 1521 did he stumble on the fact that God had dreams for him and needed him. So he abandoned his courtier life, and as a destitute pilgrim he walked some twelve thousand kilometres of the unpaved roads of Europe, always trying to follow God's beckoning. For eleven years, from 1524 to 1535, he studied arts and theology, without knowing where this would take him, though he acknowledges that God kept on trying to teach him, as a schoolteacher teaches a child. He was ordained a priest only at forty-six, and for his last fifteen years, 1541–56, he was the first superior of the Jesuit Order. But the Jesuit Order was not his only legacy to the world, for throughout his mature years he was quietly developing a spirituality – a way of living out his life before God – that would prove relevant for persons of any time, place or circumstance. Were the Jesuit Order to be suppressed again, as it was between 1773 and 1814, Ignatian spirituality would continue to thrive as Ignatius's second great legacy to humankind.

Ignatian spirituality has a perennial appeal because most of us struggle for meaning as Ignatius did, and his insights can become ours too. Although Ignatius's story is interesting in itself, more important is the fact that his personal experiences have a universal resonance. As the Introduction to the Penguin Classics 2004 edition of Ignatius's *Personal Writings* says: 'His influence on the development of spiritual awareness has been unique.' His own spiritual awareness began at thirty when he stopped to think and began to attend to the play of the movements of his heart. He noticed that certain thoughts and images were sustaining and brought him lasting joy and energy, whereas others left him feeling dry and discontented. He interpreted the first set as coming from that life-giving and sustaining source whom we call God, who endlessly draws us to life, joy, peace and purpose. It was at this point that his life took off: God had emerged from the shadows, and from then on Ignatius tried to keep God before his eyes and to notice God's leadings. This spiritual awareness can also grow in *you* because Ignatian spirituality is centred not on a set of pious practices or on Ignatius himself, but on meeting God in your personal experience. This is spiritual awareness: you allow yourself to be encountered by God in the messy, changing and often absurd world in which you live. The impact of encountering God is transforming: it brings inner joy and peace, and also opens you up to horizons of compassion and concern for your world.

This book offers an introduction to the key realities that shaped Ignatius's life and forged his spirituality. It is an abridgement of a far longer work, Tellechea Idigoras's *Ignatius the Pilgrim Saint*. I was attracted by this author's approach to Ignatius, both as a Basque and as a non-Jesuit. As a Basque portraying the most famous of his own countrymen, he has a unique insight into Ignatius's world-view. As a diocesan priest and a highly reputed medieval historian, he takes a fresh and independent stance before his subject, which enables him to dispel myths and caricatures and to present Ignatius as the vibrant and attractive personality that he was. I undertook this abridgement in order, as Ignatius would put it, 'to help people' – especially those who might find the full-length story too daunting. 'To help people to what?' one might ask. To help them to experience the activity of God in their own lives and to respond appropriately. Those who enjoy this book are encouraged to delve into the full text of *Ignatius the Pilgrim Saint*.

With the grace of God, a fire was kindled more than five hundred years ago, a fire that continues to kindle other fires. It is good to know the beginnings of a story that has stood the test of time and is ongoing. Ignatius's adventure with God can illuminate your own, and can help you to play your own unique role in the world's development. A health warning, however, is attached! Ignatius had no time for negative criticism of the darkened world of his day: instead, as a Basque, he would ask himself: *'What should I do?'* His is not an armchair spirituality: rather, it invites you to engage with our labouring God to heal a fractured world. Since this can seem too daunting, Ignatius would ask: *'Can I help one person?'* The question posed at the end of each chapter is intended to help your personal reflection, out of which can emerge decisions, stances and actions that are in tune with God's single intention, the ultimate happiness of all humankind.

1. Fantasies and Sources

MEMORY LANE

Were Ignatius to return today to his native land, as he did in 1535 when he was forty-four years old, he would have a hard time recognising the scenes of his childhood. Azpeitia, the town nearest to Loyola, has changed hugely, but if he entered its parish church he would find the old baptismal font, now restored, and nearby an inscription in Basque, capable of shaking his soul: 'Here Ignatius of Loyola was baptised.' Wandering through the oldest section of the inner city, which today has been enlarged and surrounded by ugly factories, he would come across St Ignatius Street. He would walk out of the town in the direction of his home, and find himself in a magnificent basilica with a silver statue of himself above the main altar.

HOME AGAIN

Feeling confused by now, he might fall in line with a crowd of weary tourists on their way to visit one of the 'musts' of the tour, the *santa casa*, the Holy House. Then suddenly his heart would beat faster, because there they are – the unmistakable walls of his home, the solid rocks, the carved coat of arms and the brickwork upper storeys that his grandfather built after the King had ordered the demolition of the original towers and fortifications, as a punishment for rebellion. Two statues would be immensely suggestive: one of a knight standing erect in heavy armour, and the other of some soldiers carrying a wounded man on a litter. A dog is giving the broken warrior a warm welcome home. Ignatius would remember the dog's name and what company it was to him during his long lonely hours of convalescence. The guides would tell the tourists nothing about his family, even though they had been very prominent. Instead, everything would be about himself and his spiritual family of Jesuits.

BELONGING TO ANOTHER

Ignatius would experience another surge of emotion if he went up to the top storey of the house and looked at the statue of himself as a convalescent with his eyes raised from his book to gaze at a little wooden carving of the Blessed Virgin. This was the room where his adventure had begun. It was in this room that he had been born anew. It had been a slow, difficult birth into a life that would be directed by a compass not of his own making. The dreams he had nurtured during the long hours spent in the solitude of this room had marked his life, because from that time on he was free, his life had truly become his own, or rather his life no longer belonged to himself but to Another, to the One who would take him where he had never dreamed of going.

LEGACY

On his way to the blacksmith's house, where he had been nursed as a child, he might stop off at a fine building named The Centre of Spirituality. While at the centre, a friendly Jesuit would explain that people came there to make the Spiritual Exercises of St Ignatius. In the library, his heart would beat faster when he gazed on some familiar titles: the *Spiritual Exercises*, the *Autobiography*, *Constitutions of the Society of Jesus*. Elsewhere he would find thick volumes titled the *Narrative Sources for the Life of St Ignatius* and the *Beginnings of the Society of Jesus*. He would turn the pages of his *Spiritual Journal*, which deals with a single year of his life (1544–45) and which reveals how intense his mystical experiences were. He would see a note stating that the *Spiritual Exercises* has been edited more than 4,500 times since the first edition in 1548. He might look at the numerous biographies of himself, some sympathetic, others highly critical. He would surely shake his head in wonder at more than one hundred volumes of the *History of the Society of Jesus*, twenty-four of them dealing with himself.

THE *AUTOBIOGRAPHY*

We may now leave the world of fantasy and focus instead on the sources for the present book. Chief among these is Ignatius's *Autobiography*, dictated to a Jesuit scribe a few years before Ignatius's death in 1556 and written at the request of his Jesuit companions. For long they had begged for an account of 'how the Lord had guided him from the beginning of his conversion'. The autobiography begins abruptly with his wounding at Pamplona in 1521, and ends with his early years in Rome, where he lived from 1538 to 1556. The protagonist in the tale is not himself but God. Ignatius is the anonymous pilgrim, referred to in the third person, the one who trudges toward the unknown, guided by a fundamental trust in Him who is leading him, without knowing to what nor to where he is being led.

OTHER SOURCES

After Ignatius's death, his companion Nadal gave the Ignatian profile some cosmetic touching up and spread *his* vision of Ignatius throughout the Society of Jesus in Europe. Then in 1572 came the official image, in Pedro Ribadeneira's *Biography of St Ignatius*. This met with criticism, so another version was commissioned, which led to caustic and abusive exchanges between Maffei, its author, and Ribadeneira, all of which benefits the present-day historian.

Ignatius's beatification process began in 1596, with tribunals meeting in places linked to Ignatius to gather up the precious but fading memories of those who had known him during his life. The quotations in the pages that follow are taken either from the *Autobiography* or from persons who had known Ignatius. In 1609 he was beatified and in 1622 he was canonised along with Francis Xavier, his dearest friend, and Teresa of Avila. The mythification was at last solidified and the results would be spectacular, for this was the age of baroque art, triumphant, splendid, heroic and miraculous. Could anyone standing under the glorious vaults of the Gesu in Rome ever recognise the poor pilgrim who walked shoeless and in threadbare clothes over half of Europe?

Ignatius's life no longer belonged to himself but to Another.

If you were to return after your death to the scenes of your life, what effect would this have on you?

15

2. Family Background

LOCATION

The manor house of Loyola nestles in the middle of a wide and slightly curved valley through which flows a small river. The word Loyola itself means 'a bog'. This valley, like so many others in the region, is lost in a maze of mountains. The landscape is brilliantly green in spring and summer. In autumn, this verdant appearance takes on a golden hue mixed with the warm shades of oncoming fall, and when winter comes all becomes muted violet and rust.

Small hills rise up on one side of the Loyola manor. They are blanketed with thick groves of chestnut, beech and oak. On the other side stands the imposing limestone mountain, Mount Izarraitz. The summit offers a spectacular panorama of innumerable surrounding mountains and the immense expanse of the sea. In stormy weather, rain clouds charge in from the Bay of Biscay: then the mountain, appearing like a majestic wall, seems to take on a dark and sombre aspect that borders on the ominous. The mountain is at once heartless, magnificent, inhuman, tremendous – and almost bewitching. It is mysterious, magical, and behind it each day the sun goes to hide its rays.

COAT OF ARMS

Above the front door of Ignatius's home was a stone, upon which the ancient coat of arms of the Onaz and the Loyola families was chiselled; wolves that spoke of dominion, daring and greed, and a cauldron that seemed to have boiled down the family's past history but might be cooking up an unpredictable future. In the house were the fighting arms, well kept and polished; the casks; the farm implements; the clothes; and the utensils that contributed to making the family's inventories grow in importance. All of these were duly catalogued in various last wills and testaments.

INDEPENDENT

The house stood cautiously aloof from two nearby towns, Azpeitia and Azcoitia. Ignatius, then, was born and lived in a world isolated from urban culture, cut off both by physical space and by the distance his ancestors had imposed upon the world outside. It is for this reason that his family background takes on something more than just ordinary importance. Within this setting, Ignatius was reared. He was basically always an independent man. The hunger he later demonstrated for the hermit life was not some passing fancy. He was a man with a capacity to live alone: within the depths of his soul he longed for solitude, a solitude that came from his very nature. How else could a child who had been born in a lonesome, isolated house, surrounded by a dense grove, turn out?

THIRTEENTH AND YOUNGEST

Ignatius's parents had been married twenty-four years when he was born in 1491. He was thirty – not twenty-six as he himself thought – when his life was changed by a cannonball at Pamplona. The youngest of thirteen, he had eight brothers and four sisters, and although the Basques are considered the tallest of the Spanish people, Ignatius in contrast was very small. He was only seven years old in 1498 when Martín, his next to oldest brother and heir to the family estate, married Magdalena, and she took charge of the house of Loyola. This indicates that Ignatius's mother was already dead.

Ignatius grew up side by side with his brother's children, identifying with the adults, before whom he felt small, while distancing himself from his nephews and nieces, before whom he felt older. He also grew up among the house servants and the tenants and lessees of lands, iron works and mills.

THE ABSENT MOTHER

Ignatius had no living grandparents to dote on him, to tell him stories, to help him to get through his early life experiences and to show more tolerance toward him than did the authority figures in the household. His father died in 1507 when he was about sixteen, and shortly afterward Ignatius had left the manor house. Of his mother, nothing is known for sure except her name, Doña Marina. We do not know when she was born or died. Strangely, we do not find Ignatius making the slightest allusion anywhere to her. Did he ever have the opportunity to know her or did she always remain simply a faceless name for him? Surely the death of his mother during his childhood days must have left its indelible mark on the deepest part of his psyche, on the affective personality, that area that defines what is fundamentally human in us. He lacked, then, the protective, liberating, fostering maternal presence that would have given him early direction, basic confidence, and that would have opened up new objectives for him.

WANDERING ADVENTURER

The lack of nurturing by a mother can engender habits of depression later in life; it affects the way one reacts to and relates with others; it incites vague feelings of guilt. Some psychologists suggest that every wandering adventurer

Ignatius was basically always an independent man.

is responding to the hidden and irresolvable need to compensate for the lack of maternal nurturing, whose function is to provide a child with affective perimeters. Could this be the key to explaining why Ignatius was a wandering adventurer during the greater part of his life? Then there is the mysterious figure of the lady who occupied his thoughts during his convalescence. Was she a mother image, betraying a lack of affective development in the dreamer? In Ignatius's affections as a child, his mother was substituted for either by his wet nurse or by his sister-in-law. The wet nurse, María Garin, wife of the local blacksmith, must have played an important role in his early psychological development, and it is in her face, arms and breasts that are forever hidden those secrets that are absent from what he wrote.

Q 2

What key elements of your upbringing shape your views on life?

3. Growing Up, 1498–1506

FAITH

Perhaps Ignatius would have had the opportunity as a growing child to hold in his hand the venerable house documents, which included a bull from Benedict XIII, signed in 1415, referring to the Loyola patronage of the local village church at Azpeitia, and another from the Catholic Majesty of Spain, which spoke of his father and his 'many good and loyal services' and how he had placed his person 'in danger and peril' at the service of the Crown.

Ignatius acquired in his own home and from his earliest days a deep devotion to Mary, which he never lost. Besides the liturgical cycle, the many feast days and the local pilgrimages became part of his upbringing. A Franciscan influence was also implanted in his soul, due to the presence of Franciscan convents in the area. Like a seed, the name of Saint Francis of Assisi was sown in Ignatius's mind at an early age, and the day would come when it would blossom forth to enlighten his spirit.

FEUDS

But despite these honourable deeds and the Christian culture of the times, feuds and discords were at the very heart of the Loyola family heritage. Sin as well as faith was part of the legacy bequeathed to Ignatius: there were two illegitimate children within Ignatius's own family. In the last wills and testaments of his ancestors, there is not a trace of sorrow for what resulted from their ferocious hatreds and terrible vendettas, but there is evidence enough of their ardent desire to make up for lost time, to look for penitential atonement for whatever was incompatible with personal responsibility. The protection and salvation of their souls was an obsession with them, and this was long before Ignatius would write his famous phrase in the *Spiritual Exercises*: 'and by this manner to save one's soul'. His brother Martín, the heir of Loyola, conscious of his 'enormous sins', would seek help at his death from 'the immaculate Queen of the angels' and would bequeath much to her hermitages.

NEW HORIZONS

The world of Ignatius's adolescence was peopled with foreign names, faraway monarchs and wars. Europe and the discoveries of the New World became familiar to him through his kinsfolk and countrymen. It was a Basque who would be the first to circumnavigate the world in 1522. His sister-in-law Magdalena would have told him about Queen Isabella, in whose service she had been and who would surely have given her some very beautiful books, including perhaps *The Life of Christ* and *The Flower of the Saints*. Notions of courage and loyalty, of service, honour and fame, were beginning to take shape in his impressionable mind.

While Ignatius kept up his reading and writing lessons at home, he also revisited the local blacksmith. He watched his nurse's husband Martín as he stirred up the fire, laid the red-hot iron flat on the anvil, hammered it with swift, hard, well-aimed blows until it took the shape of a hoe, a weapon or a horseshoe. The blacksmith alone determined what the metal was going to be. 'See that?' Martín would ask laconically. *Seeing, knowing how to see, was enough for Ignatius to learn the power of action, with its hard, resistant, lasting results.* This was one lesson that remained imprinted on his soul, a lesson that appealed to him more than learning how to trace out letters with a goose quill. 'We stay here,' continued the blacksmith tersely, 'but the iron is to go to England, Flanders … to soldiers too … perhaps to your brothers far away.'

HERE OR FAR AWAY?

By temperament, Ignatius was hungry for adventure and achievement. This factor, plus the force of necessity due to his low status in the household, compelled him to consider the alternatives of remaining in a dead end at Loyola or of seeking his fortune elsewhere. His father was anxious to provide for his last son, and shortly before he died he brought it about that no less a person than the Chief Treasurer of the realm would open the doors of his home to Ignatius and receive him as a son. The Treasurer's wife was a relative of the Loyolas. In this household at Arévalo, Ignatius would be educated, and from there it would not be difficult for him to obtain a position at court.

And so on a certain day in the year 1506, when Ignatius was fifteen, he left Loyola's green valley for Arévalo. He would have felt the reassuring hand of his father on his shoulder as he departed, and at the same time he would have felt his mother's absence. His father would go to his rest peacefully a year later, on 23 October 1507. Ignatius was then all alone, but he was well situated to take on whatever the future had in store for him.

ARÉVALO

As Ignatius made his way through Burgos toward Arévalo, around him were vast Castilian fields that resembled a sea of gold, making the Loyola holdings seem like small garden plots in comparison. His proud, well-built house stood humble and unassuming against the palaces of Castile's leading families.

The Chief Treasurer, Velázquez, and his wife María, truly welcomed Ignatius as a son. His new home was in every respect a Royal Palace, and the family was then basking in dazzling prosperity and glory. The children would have told him that their father was a personal friend of King Ferdinand, that he had the King's confidence, and that he had profited from his many favours. Queen Isabella had paid frequent visits to Arévalo, and the children's grandfather had served her for thirty years.

In this large family that numbered six sons and six daughters, Ignatius once again became number thirteen. His insertion into the family circle posed no problem because the difference in ages among his peers was not great. Although he fitted easily into the daily regime of studies and recreation, the process of adjusting to a new and different kind of life would have been more difficult for him. For the next ten years until he was twenty-five, he breathed an atmosphere of luxury and sumptuous riches. This was the worst start imaginable for his future life, a fact that makes his adult choice of extreme poverty so much more challenging.

The world of Ignatius's adolescence was peopled with foreign names, faraway monarchs and wars.

How did choices you made in your adolescent years shape your future?

4. The Courtly Life, 1506-17

VALIANT KNIGHT

Ignatius's father had requested of Spain's Chief Treasurer Velázquez 'that he might give him one of his sons so that he might receive him in his home and help him through his favour', and later on might introduce him at court. In his *Autobiography,* Ignatius alludes to 'the time when he served at the court of the Catholic Monarchs'. He was not a genuine page, although the sons of Velázquez were, while the daughters were ladies-in-waiting. But on various occasions during Ignatius's years at Arévalo, King Ferdinand stayed for days and even weeks there. Ignatius would then have played the role of junior page and would have experienced awe in the presence of the Spanish monarch. His presentation at court would have proceeded somewhat as follows:

> 'Your Majesty, this is the youngest son of Don Beltram de Loyola.'
> 'Indeed, what has become of your father?'
> 'He died in October 1507, your Majesty.'
> 'He was a loyal vassal, a valiant knight, and he conducted himself bravely at Burgos and Fuenterrabía. And Doña Magdalena?'
> 'She married my brother Martín, your Majesty, and is living at my home in Loyola.'

Those magic terms 'loyal vassal' and 'valiant knight', coming from the monarch's lips in reference to his father, would have enchanted and dazzled Ignatius. It meant more to be called a vassal by a great king than to be the petty lord and chief of the clans back home.

DREAMS

Ignatius's field of vision quickly became much wider than it had been at Loyola. Each piece of news was a tempting challenge: the alliances and wars of emperors and kings, the conquering of Cuba in 1510 and of Florida in 1511, and the discovery of the Pacific Ocean in 1513. There was also a great deal of talk about the new University of Alcalá, but the world of letters held no attraction for Ignatius. In the Basque mind, the man determined to make his mark on the world had three choices: 'The Church, the sea, or the court.'

Ignatius was thrilled by the refined court music and wanted to learn to play musical instruments. He was interested also in books dealing with chivalry, and the older boys would secretly pass these on to him. Battles, tournaments, famous exploits, feats of glory: he would identify with the brilliant image he had dreamed up for himself, one in which he would surpass all other valiant knights. And again, what about the lady fair who was so essential in the life of every knight, the 'woman of his thoughts and mistress of his heart?' At the very least, she had to be 'very beautiful, generous and virtuous'. When and how did Ignatius choose that inaccessible woman? Was she in fact the Infanta Catalina of Austria, who would one day become the consort of King John III of Portugal, a woman referred to as 'the most beautiful creature in the world'?

THE PRODIGAL

Little by little, Ignatius began to forget Loyola. He started to distance himself from his homeland, physically and spiritually. Like every prodigal son, he had left 'for a distant country', drunk with the present and casting the past aside like a tattered garment. However, he returned at least once from Arévalo to Loyola, and he left behind him an unpleasant memory. He was now an outsider, a conceited, arrogant young man who was used to rubbing shoulders with the high and mighty in Arévalo. During Mardi Gras in 1515, accompanied by his brother Pedro, the priest in the Loyola family, he engaged at Loyola in some nocturnal misdemeanours, which, according to the court records, were 'premeditated and enormous crimes'.

These wrongdoings, it was alleged, took place 'at night and deliberately, as a result of a conversation during which ambush and treachery were pre-arranged'. Nowhere do we find a precise definition of what these misdeeds entailed, but the crime led to the intervention of the Provincial Magistrate. As soon as what he had done was discovered, Ignatius fled to Pamplona, where he sought episcopal protection under the pretext that he was a cleric. Once there, he was arrested and confined to the episcopal prison. The Church did come to his aid but the magistrate pressed charges against Ignatius and claimed that he was a lay man and not a cleric, since his name had never been inscribed in the registers of Pamplona and he had never worn the prescribed clerical garb.

A DASHING YOUNG MAN

With the obvious intention of emphasising the lay, even worldly character of Ignatius, the magistrate brilliantly put together a set of notes that throw light on the impression that the young Loyola courtier made on people at the time. The magistrate pointed out that it was well known that far from wearing ecclesiastical dress, Ignatius had for months, and even years, been carrying arms and wearing a wide-open cape, and that his hair, styled shoulder length,

'You will not learn nor become wise until someone breaks your leg.'

gave no outward sign of having been cut in the manner prescribed for clerics. He depicts for us an Ignatius bedecked in clothing designed with multicoloured checked materials, a red cap – the distinctive mark of his family – a sword fastened to his belt, wearing a metal breastplate and other knightly accoutrements, and clutching onto his crossbow. Then, dipping his brush in shadier hues, the magistrate added that this youth was involved in worldly pursuits in a way that belied clerical decorum, both in his dress and even more in his morals. Whether or not the young Loyola had told the truth about his clerical status cannot be proven, but it is clear that he had had recourse to the Church in order to escape his responsibilities, a poor start for a man who one day would be counted among the illustrious 'men of the Church'.

'UNTIL SOMEONE BREAKS YOUR LEG'
The magistrate lost his case and Ignatius hurried as fast as he could back to Arévalo, where he bragged about his adventures and his escape. This was the first warning signal for this young man who was so full of self-assurance. At Arévalo, there would be more forebodings, specifically a warning from his good old aunt, a nun: 'Ignatius, you will not learn nor become wise until someone breaks your leg.' She had no way of knowing that what she spoke was a premonition. All of this happened in 1515, when he was twenty-four. In January 1516, King Ferdinand died, Charles I ascended the Spanish throne, and suddenly Ignatius's life changed dramatically and disastrously.

Q4
What embarrassing episodes helped to shape your young adult life?

5. Ignatius in Navarre, 1517-21

LEFT WITHOUT A PATRON

In 1516, the new Spanish monarch, Charles I, gave as a gift to Queen Germaine, the widow of his predecessor, all the revenues and rights that the Chief Treasurer Velázquez had held. The Velázquez family were immediately ruined, stripped of their offices and evicted from their home. The situation was disastrous not only for the family, but for Ignatius. In the following year, 1517, Velázquez died 'without having been able to leave Ignatius well-placed'. This was the cause of a bitter awakening for Ignatius. María, Velázquez's widow, was generous and she sought out a new, powerful protector for him, a man also related to the Loyolas. After giving Ignatius two horses and the tidy sum of five hundred gold coins, she sent him off with letters of introduction to his new prospective patron's household.

Thus his ambition to be a courtier had been dashed to pieces. There was nothing else open to him but the life of a professional man in the service of another, even though his soul and body had been stamped with the fine polished manners of the court. He would always carry himself with a certain dignity and elegance that he could never conceal, even in the disguise of a beggar's rags. Toward the end of the century, when the cause of his beatification was introduced, there were women who could still remember the beggar's gentle comportment and his delicate hands. But as of now, he would have to begin over again by becoming the satellite of the Viceroy of Navarre, Don Antonio. To return to Loyola would have been too humiliating for him.

SERVING THE VICEROY OF NAVARRE

Navarre had been an independent kingdom tucked away in the Pyrenees since the time of Charlemagne. But between 1512 and 1515, it was appropriated by the King of Spain, and a viceroy was appointed. Ignatius's request for employment in the service of the newly named viceroy was granted. The latter received him as a gentleman and regarded him as 'a member of his household.' Thus, although Ignatius was adept in handling a sword when necessity called for it, he was not formally a soldier.

'IGNATIUS WOULD HAVE KILLED'

Ignatius spent over three years as a gentleman of the vice-regal household, and during most of this time he remained in Pamplona and was despised as part of the occupation forces. Many years later, the Viceroy's brother would recall with tears the day when a crowd of men met Ignatius in a narrow street and pressed him up against a wall. Ignatius unsheathed his sword and ran down the street after his unknown attackers. The witness to this scene was a friend of Ignatius, a man who 'had known him for a long time at his home', and he stated, 'if someone had not stopped him, Ignatius would have killed one of them, or one of them would have killed him'. Was it an example of sterling courage on Ignatius's part or perhaps fear in action? We do not know.

THE WOMAN OF HIS DREAMS

The young Infanta Catalina of Austria attended tournaments performed in 1518 in Valladolid, at which Ignatius was also present. Committed to the care of her deranged mother, who had been locked up, Catalina was thus a prisoner herself, but she had been freed for a few hours to witness these events. To men like Ignatius, who were in the habit of reading romantic novels, Catalina's tender and singular beauty, enhanced by her rich attire and her condition as an inaccessible lady held in captivity, made her an object of chivalrous dreams. Did he see her in 1518? Was she 'the lady of his thoughts'? We do not know. He only tells us that 'the lady was not of the lesser nobility, nor was she a countess, nor a duchess; her station was much higher than any of these'. Later, as indicated above, Catalina became the consort of King John III of Portugal.

THREATENED WITH DEATH

Among the thousands of pieces of correspondence that passed to and from the King's Chancellery, one, recently discovered, interests us in a special way: 'All Powerful Lord: Iñigo Lopez de Loyola [Ignatius] declares that he has a difference and disagreement with a Gallician, Francisco del Hoyo. He says that this man wants to kill him and is looking for the opportunity to put his resolution into effect, that he has often pursued him, and that he had never accepted reconciliation, despite the fact that it has been offered to him [by Ignatius] many times. For this reason the said Iñigo has great need to carry arms to safeguard and defend his person, as he will explain to you if necessary. He begs Your Highness to grant him the right to bear the said arms; on his part, he offers surety that he will not engage or offend anyone else with these arms. He will be most grateful if Your Highness will grant him his request.'

Authorisation was given in 1518 to Ignatius to carry arms as requested, and it was renewed in 1519 and 1520. The original incident that prompted this royal concession went back to the time when Ignatius was living in Arévalo.

A LOVE AFFAIR?

May we suspect that this desire for revenge, so tenacious and relentless, on the part of Hoyo, makes sense only in the context of a love affair, a triangle in which the woman this time was not the inaccessible lady of Ignatius's dreams, but the wife or daughter of Hoyo? Years later, when Ignatius writes in the *Exercises* of the scheming of the devil, he says that he can be compared to a false lover who seeks to remain hidden and does not want to be discovered. If such a lover speaks with evil intention to the daughter of a good father, or to the wife of a good husband, and seeks to seduce them, he wants his words and solicitations kept secret. He is greatly displeased if his evil suggestions and depraved intentions are revealed by the daughter to her father or by the wife to her husband, for he then readily sees he will not succeed in what he had begun.

Could it be that in this excerpt from the *Exercises* Ignatius is speaking from personal experience, and that Hoyo was a good husband or a good father, whom Ignatius had offended by trying to seduce his wife or daughter?

'If someone had not stopped him, Ignatius would have killed one of them, or one of them would have killed him.'

Recall incidents in which you followed your instincts and where they led you.

6. Wounded in Pamplona, 1521

THE STRUGGLE FOR NAVARRE

Since the kingdom of Navarre was seen as the key to control of Spain, both France and Spain were determined to possess it. Ignatius's master, the Spanish Viceroy in Navarre, saw that an attack by French forces seemed likely, and so he accelerated construction of a new fortress in Pamplona in Navarre. As it happened, in 1516 the greater part of the castle where Francis Xavier lived was demolished and reduced to an ordinary dwelling manor, as a punishment for the family's support of the Navarrese, and the solid beams from this house were used in the building of the new fortress. By the beginning of 1518, it was manned by a permanent garrison and stocked as an armoury.

Two years later, an insurgency against Spanish rule was brutally repressed by the Viceroy, with imprisonment, confiscation of property, executions and a horrible pillage of the town 'according to the practice of war'. Ignatius was in the Viceroy's army. He had fought and won but he did not want to participate in the pillaging. 'Even though he could have taken a large part of the booty, it seemed to him of little value, and he never wanted to take the smallest bit.' His was a small gesture of decency on that inglorious day, 18 September 1520.

THE SIEGE OF PAMPLONA

In the spring of 1521, the fortress of Pamplona and some local castles sent out calls to the Spanish throne for help. But the King of Spain had his own problems, and troops from Pamplona were sent to Castile instead, leaving Pamplona in worse shape than ever. In mid-May, the French army began to march south. From the French point of view, the issue was the liberation of Navarre from Spain. From the Spanish perspective, the French were guilty of an invasion of Spanish territory. On 16 May 1521, the French army made its appearance a half a league from Pamplona. Panic ensued, and the Viceroy fled to seek reinforcements and to save his life. Supporters of Spain also fled, with the result that, by 18 May, Pamplona was helpless and on the verge of becoming a ghost town.

The town council requested that the command of the city be turned over to them so that they could negotiate with the French. At this critical moment, the first Spanish reinforcements arrived under the command of Ignatius's brother, Martín. Ignatius met his brother on the outskirts of Pamplona, and the Loyolas demanded that they be entrusted with the command of the remaining Spanish garrison, but the town council refused this. Martín, wild with bitterness and anger, retired with his troops, but Ignatius felt that to abandon the city would be shameful. With a few supporters, he galloped into Pamplona. 'He judged it disreputable to retreat.' In time, Ignatius would write in his *Exercises* that 'shame and fear for one's good name in the eyes of the world' would instead be obstacles for the person who strives to serve God freely.

DEFENCE OF THE IMPOSSIBLE

In 1553, when dictating his *Autobiography,* Ignatius told of the impetuous gesture that was his and his alone. 'He was in a fortress that the French were attacking, and although all the others saw clearly that they could not defend themselves and were of the opinion that they should surrender, provided their lives were spared, he gave so many reasons to the commander that at last he persuaded him to defend it. This was contrary to the views of all the knights, but they were energised by his courage and gallantry.' The city of Pamplona could not be defended effectively, but the fortress might, and Ignatius's heroism was contagious. On the following day, the magnificent French army marched into the city and it welcomed the two flags of France and Navarre. The fortress was the last place of resistance. Ignatius 'gave his opinion that they should not surrender, but that they should defend or die'. And then 'when the day arrived on which they expected the bombardment, he confessed his sins to one of his companions-in-arms'. The sins of his lifetime were weighing heavily on him. When he poured out his conscience to his surprised confessor, the latter with some astonishment learned more about the hidden and unsuspected facets of the personality of his proud penitent than he did about the man's serious, but run-of-the-mill, sins.

SERIOUSLY WOUNDED

'After the bombardment by the French had been going on for some time, a cannonball struck him on one leg, crushing its bones, and because it passed between his legs the other was also seriously wounded. Shortly after he fell, the defenders of the fortress surrendered to the French....' This was Ignatius's own precise account of 20 May and the event that was to change his life.

Ignatius may have lain wounded and helpless for several days in one of the corners of the fortress before the terms of a ceasefire were agreed. In that interval, he would have received inadequate emergency care as he waited feverishly for the victor's arrival, and he may well have embarked on the road

Ignatius's life could be summed up in two words – running away.

that led within. He would have had to contemplate his whole past, like every prodigal son who must retreat within himself to find himself and to examine the long road that had led to his self-estrangement. Perhaps his intuition told him that ever since those intoxicating days at Arévalo, his life could be summed up in two words: running away. Had he not been, in the words of St Augustine, a stubborn 'fugitive from his own heart'? Would he have felt a new kind of shame – the shame of vain honour, of the emptiness of life, the numbness of his dormant faith? At this moment, in a corner of Pamplona's fortress, he must have remembered his old aunt's prediction: 'Iñigo, you will never learn or become wise until someone breaks your leg!'

Q6

How has illness changed your life?

Wounded at Pamplona

7. Convalescence at Loyola, 1521-22

THE JOURNEY HOME

When the victorious French soldiers took over the citadel of Pamplona, 'they found Ignatius lying on the ground and they brought him into the town, because many knew him there, and his own enemies exerted themselves in taking care of him, providing him with doctors and the rest, until it seemed best to send him home, so that during his convalescence, which would be long, he would be better off'. Ignatius, therefore, was a privileged casualty of the war. He repaid the civility of his adversaries by presenting them with his buckler, dagger and cuirass. After giving him preliminary care over a two-week period, they put him on a litter and brought him home. Even though the countrymen-turned-litter-bearers carried him with great care, his journey home was physically agonising. Feelings of shame and confusion must also have tortured his soul. He showed uncommon strength and courage in the face of suffering, and to this attribute was added another: in the midst of all his pain 'he did not show himself hateful toward anyone and he did not blaspheme God'.

[handwritten margin note: he seems to have alot of knock on his side]

BUTCHERY

Ignatius arrived back at Loyola in early June 1521. His brother would have upbraided him for his lunacy at Pamplona, while his sister-in-law Doña Magdalena would have nursed him quietly and with gentle care. Because his sufferings were unbearably persistent, as is normally the case with bone injuries, he did not feel like engaging in the small talk that ordinarily follows the kind of adventure he had been through. His right knee, which had been shattered, began to get worse, either because the bones were not set properly at Pamplona or because they had become dislocated during the journey home. Several doctors and surgeons were summoned and all were of the same opinion: the bones had to be reset or they would never heal properly.

Many years afterward, Ignatius talked about this extremely painful operation. 'And again he went through this butchery, and during it, as in all other operations he had undergone, he uttered no word nor showed any sign of pain other than to clench his fists.' He was by nature a man of incalculable inner strength.

A WASTED LIFE

Despite the best care available, Ignatius's condition worsened; he could not eat and 'the symptoms that normally foretell death' began to appear. On 24 June, the feast of St John, 'he was advised to make his confession'. He received the sacraments and thereby validated his hasty confession at Pamplona. Once again he was forced to make an appraisal of his life, but this time it was done peacefully, without pressure. It may have been that many idols crashed noisily to the ground during this hour that he could have considered his last, but we do not know because he is silent on what took place. But later in life, in speaking with his companions, he would refer to the bad habits that he used to have. We may indicate some of these as follows.

From the first lines of the *Autobiography*, we know that until 1521 'he was a man given up to the pleasures of the world, and, motivated by a strong and vain desire to win renown, he took special delight in the exercise of arms'. His delight in the vanity of arms was limited to tournaments, duels and challenges of honour. He further admits that 'he had been much given to reading worldly and fictitious books which are generally known as tales of chivalry....'

More seriously, Polanco, his secretary in his later years, tells us that his life until 1521 was far from being spiritual: 'He was very free when it came to loving women, gambling, and quarrelling about personal honour.' Elsewhere, Polanco states: 'Even though he had an affection for the faith, he did not live it, nor did he avoid sin; rather, he was particularly wayward in gambling, womanising, quarrelling, and in matters of arms.'

Thus we are given a picture of how Ignatius had wasted away his youth. His faith was neither alive nor operative; his life was not integrated. He was restless, rebellious, and dissipated in vices, especially sensuality. Gambling, womanising and brawling were the customs of the times, and his style of life mirrored that of his peers. His exploits reveal moral bankruptcy. Laínez, his successor as General of the Society, tells the story without palliatives when he says that Ignatius 'was attacked and defeated by the vices of the flesh'.

EMBERS OF FAITH

Even in a person who has led a most dissolute life, living embers of the faith can survive, and these hidden resources are capable of regenerating what was once in evidence. We know of three things that Ignatius had held onto during his destructive early life. First, he did not partake in the pillaging of a conquered town in 1518 because 'it seemed to him an undignified thing to do'. Second, although blasphemy was a common vice in those days, Ignatius never blasphemed, not even when he was suffering the greatest pain. Finally, he never hated anyone, neither his rivals in his affairs of honour nor his enemies in times of war. These three facts are clues to his interior disposition, but it is only when the pandemonium of life is stilled that one can hear the voices that are never quiet. God does not speak to us until we are capable of creating a silence within ourselves.

AN UNCERTAIN FUTURE

Ignatius made his confession and received Communion, but his physical condition became critical. On 28 June 1521, the vigil of the Feast of St Peter, to whom he had a great devotion, the physicians stated that 'If he did not get better by midnight, he could consider himself as good as dead'. But that very night he began to improve and was soon out of danger, and once again he returned to his vain illusions. He would have heard how the French and Navarrese had overrun the frontier castles of Navarre, and of the dismissal of his master, the Viceroy of the King of Spain, which left Ignatius again without a protector, since his loyalty was with the King. All he had now was his honour and the consolation that he was not declared a rebel, whereas the brothers of Francis Xavier were, because of their support for the Navarrese in their struggle against Spain.

He was particularly wayward in gambling, womanising, quarrelling, and in matters of arms.

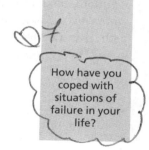

How have you coped with situations of failure in your life?

8. 'He sometimes stopped to think', 1521

RENEWED BUTCHERY

During the latter half of 1521, Ignatius's greatest concern was how to repair the poorly set bones in his knee 'because the bone protruded so much that it was an ugly sight. He was unable to abide it because he was determined to follow a worldly career and he judged his leg would be unsightly, so he asked the surgeons if they could cut off the protrusion'. His brother Martín was horrified, but Ignatius 'was determined, nevertheless, to undergo this martyrdom to gratify his own inclinations' and 'with his customary patience' he suffered the filing down of the knobbed bone. The surgeons then tried to avoid making his bad leg shorter than the other by applying ointments and stretching it with weights 'which caused him many days of martyrdom'. He finally recovered completely, but he could not put any weight on his bad leg, and so 'he had to remain in bed'. To pass away the time, he asked for some tales of chivalry 'to which he was very much addicted'.

DIFFERENT BOOKS

'Since none of the books he was accustomed to reading could be found in the house, they gave him a *Life of Christ* and a book on the *Lives of the Saints*.' Thus it was that Ignatius, who had dreamed of accomplishing great deeds and had opted for martyrdom to correct a physical defect, was now introduced to new types of exploits and different kinds of martyrdom. He was introduced to flesh and blood saints, followers of 'the eternal prince, Jesus Christ, the gentle captain of their souls'. This was religious chivalry and they were 'the knights of God'. Such a description resonated stealthily in Ignatius's imagination. He began to conjure up images of a different king, of another kingdom, of knights who were not fictional but historical role-models with whom he could identify. He was a man obsessed with meeting challenges and with 'being more', and so now he began to consider this new stimulating interest in terms of a challenge, and he became more involved in what he was reading.

PUTTING HIS READING ASIDE

Sometimes 'putting his reading aside, he stopped to think about the things that he had read'. For Ignatius, thinking was almost tantamount to action. As his admiration for the saints increased, a desire to do something similar began to grow in him. The moment to say Yes had not yet come, because he had yet to pull away from the deepest part of his conscious interior. As Bernanos observed, the first step toward conversion is taken in the silence at the deepest part of one's being, in that silence which youth fears and rejects.

THE POWER OF PAIN

The Pamplona event in itself did not convert Ignatius, but it created what psychology sees as a favourable framework for a radical re-evaluation of one's life. Death had grazed him, but it was physical suffering, relentlessly digging her talons into his flesh over a number of weeks, that produced the deepest impression. The French novelist Leon Bloy observed that 'Human beings have recesses in their hearts that were not there until pain came along to create them'.

CONVERSION

Conversion is a unique experience, much like the experience of being born or dying. Some conversions are intellectual, the conclusion of reasoning; others come about through the appropriation of great ideals; yet others are the fruit of emotion, of irrepressible enthusiasm or of a flashing vision of sheer beauty. Rather than being the master of one's conversion, one is conquered by it and seduced by truth, goodness or beauty. Conversion involves an integration of dispersed inner forces, which point the person in a new direction, and toward Another who is God. It involves a level of renunciation of which not all are capable. The French essayist André Gide confessed: 'I have never been able to renounce anything; I have lived a disjointed life, protecting within myself the best and the worst.'

Ignatius, who had been concentrating on nothing more than adjusting the bones of his battered knee, ended up by adjusting his disintegrated soul and his disjointed life. In the second operation, the surgeons had to saw away a number of protuberances, while the patient had to nurse his soul and renounce his will. It was a long and delicate process. He lived this first critical moment in perfect and complete solitude, and took no one into his confidence. Thirty years later, however, he would describe what had taken place then with a vividness that differed not a bit from a description of what he was living through at the moment. He could not have acted otherwise, for converts agree that what takes place at that

'Human beings have recesses in their hearts that were not there until pain came along to create them.'

moment is comparable to a second and definitive birth, the clarity of which makes one's prior history seem insignificant and empty.

Can you identify key moments in the integration of your life around God?

Convalescence at Loyola

9. Conflicting Dreams

TAKING STOCK

Let us recreate the scene in which a great change took place in Ignatius. For nine long months, from June 1521 until February 1522, he lived shut away within the upper storey of the Loyola manor house. During the course of those long weeks, he played host to physical pain, serious reading, peaceful silence and reflection; to old ambitions and impossible dreams; and to a preoccupation with what he would do in the future. Enforced inactivity helped him to take stock of what his life had been up until then and it brought back to him his childhood days. He would have retraced his thirty years and looked at all the differences they had brought. His reveries were made easier by the almost maternal care of Doña Magdalena, the daily contact with his brothers, nieces and nephews, and the rediscovery of his forgotten home, with its daily routine, customs, noises and odours, and also by the weather and landscape of his native land.

Because? his aged 30 yr

EMPTY YEARS

With thirty years behind him, Ignatius had very little to show, as far as lasting and tangible goals were concerned. Pamplona had been a suicidal, noble deed, but one in which he had been true to his own principles and to his temporal King. However, his was an unrequited loyalty, for he had been left unpaid and unthanked for what he had done. He had received no commendations; his name did not appear on the list of those singled out for merit, nor was he compensated for his wounds, because he was not a regular soldier. He had come out of this event with his honour alone and the credit he had gained in the eyes of his master, the Viceroy, who was now reduced to the status of Duke of Nájera. Ignatius could always have been assured of a post and a salary in the Duke's household, and probably even a position as the overseer of one of his castles. But what would such a poor future mean to someone like himself, who dreamed great dreams and was capable of falling in love with a princess?

ROMANTIC FANTASIES

Ignatius was not an embittered man given to resentment or scepticism. He had not given up on his life and, more remarkably, he kept unaltered his ability to dream fantastic dreams. He was not yet a convert; he was simply a convalescent whose health, together with his dormant and far-from-dead illusions, was growing stronger each day. In his daydreams, he was still given to the things of the world 'that he used to think about before'. He was neither defeated nor dejected. Who could have guessed what his thoughts were at this period of his life unless he himself, as an old man, had revealed them to us in words that seem to rekindle the glowing, tender thoughts of the past: 'Of the many vain things that came into his mind, one took such hold of his heart that he would spend two or three hours at a time absorbed in thinking about it. He dreamed about what he would do in the service of a certain lady, the means he would take to go to the land where she lived, the clever sayings and words he would speak to her, and the deeds of gallantry he would do in her service. He became so wrapped up in these fantasies that he would not even consider that it would be impossible to put them into effect, for the lady was not of the lesser nobility, nor was she a countess, nor a duchess, but her station was much higher than any of these.' How can biographers say that Ignatius, who could be 'engrossed, for two, three or four hours at a time' thinking about his lady love without noticing the time passing, was a rigid man, calculating and cold, a man impervious to love and steeled against affection?

GOD ENTERS
Since his fixation was so firmly set, so sweet, how was it possible that another idea was able to open a breach into his dream? The answer is that this new notion was empowered by the arm of God, who would shake him, 'bringing it about that these thoughts were followed by others that arose from the things he had been reading'. Since when can a book blur and blot out a woman's face? This new idea was not like a frontal attack, but more like an entrenchment dug under the foundations of the fortress and which would eventually undermine it. While reading *The Life of Christ* and *The Flower of the Saints,* 'he sometimes stopped to think' about such things. To stop and think in this way is to attend and answer, to debate and struggle within oneself.

Ignatius had always been susceptible to the fascination exercised by heroic role-models. His admiration for them was now transformed into imaginary emulation. Reflecting on what he had been reading, he began to say to himself: 'If Saint Dominic did this, I ought to do it, and if Saint Francis did that, I ought to do it.' At this stage, sanctity for Ignatius consisted in *having to do* something hard and difficult.

RESTLESS OR JOYFUL

We should not be surprised that Ignatius's enslavement between contrary desires should have exhausted him. With a master stroke of phenomenology, he describes how he was surprised by something in the very fine anatomy of these projected desires. Worldly daydreams delighted him as long as he entertained them, but when 'he grew weary of them', he put them aside only to discover that he 'was dry and restless'. On the other hand, while he thought of what he would do in pursuit of sanctity – 'of going barefoot to Jerusalem, of eating nothing but vegetables, and in imitating the saints in all the rigours that they had undergone' – he found he was consoled as long as these thoughts remained; and even afterward, when he was not thinking about them any longer, 'he remained happy and joyful'.

he grew weary of & worldly daydreams while he remained happy ~ joyful in pursuit of sanctity

#9

> Ignatius dreamed about what he would do in the service of a certain lady.

> Do you notice contradictory moods when you are struggling to make a decision?

10. The Touch of God

REFLECTION ON EXPERIENCE

The alternation of ideals in the convalescent Ignatius – feats of valour in the service of a lady and then feats of valour in competing with the saints – was followed by a change in the state of his soul, but he did not notice the subtle contrast until one day when 'his eyes were partially opened and he began to wonder at this difference'. This meant opening his eyes to the flow of his spirit and allowing himself to be won over by the surprising discovery of different reverberations that issued from the depths of his being.

Wonder, for Ignatius, was followed by reflection, and from reflection came verification. His experience was clear and precise: 'From experience he knew that some thoughts left him sad, while others made him happy.' Reflecting on this experience, he learned a lesson that he never forgot: he discovered that 'different spirits were moving in him'. His early biographer Ribadeneira emphasises the point when he informs us that 'Ignatius understood that there were two different spirits, not only different, but completely and totally opposed to one another'. He contrasted them as light and darkness, truth and falsehood, Christ and the devil. The two spirits seemed to entice him from without, and the two tendencies that began to take shape within were associated with his fantasies. God was not challenging him personally, for God as yet was far off, not personalised or intimate. Yet, at this point of his labouring reflection, God was indeed raising him onto the first rung of his upward journey and was teaching him a lesson, the consequences of which would be momentous.

INNER CLARITY

According to an off-the-record note that Gonçalves da Câmara scribbled on the margin of the autobiographical papers Ignatius was dictating to him thirty years later, Ignatius clearly saw then what were the origins of these contrary tensions. 'This was the first reflection he made on the things of God; and later on, when he was composing the Exercises, it was from this experience within himself that he began to draw light on what pertained to the diversity of spirits.'

The discovery of tensions that came about as a result of the duality of spirits, forces and desires was a great lesson for Ignatius and it provided him with 'no little light'. It was a light that clarified for him the cause of his present waverings, and, at the same time, it illuminated the darker corners of his past. 'He began to think more seriously about his past life, and he realised the great need he had to do penance for it.' 'Without giving any consideration to his present circumstance, he promised to do, with God's grace, what the saints had done.'

ON FIRE WITH GOD

All Ignatius wanted to do then was to go to Jerusalem as soon as he became well, in order, as he said, 'to observe all the fasts and to practise all the disciplines any generous soul on fire with God usually wants to do'. His ancestors had been accustomed, at the moment of their death, to ask that someone make a 'pilgrimage for their soul to far off Holy Places'. Ignatius wanted to make his own pilgrimage himself. Why Jerusalem? In his *Life of Christ*, Ludolph the Carthusian declared that there was 'no sight more delightful than seeing with the eyes of the body and contemplating with the powers of the soul the land where Christ earned our redemption'. Jerusalem was the land of Jesus. Because of its great distance, it was seen as symbolising a rupture with the past and, perhaps and most importantly, it represented a quest – the unconscious call to the faraway ethereal place.

OUR LADY'S VISIT

In a wonderful understatement, Ignatius noted that 'it seemed that all the fantasies he had previously pictured in his mind gradually faded away before the holy desires he now had....' Then came an inner support, which he called a 'visitation', and many years later he described it with matter-of-fact frankness. It would be impossible to improve on his own rendition of it in the *Autobiography*: 'One night, as he lay sleepless, he clearly saw the likeness of our Lady with the Holy Child Jesus. From this vision he received great consolation for a remarkably long time. He felt so great a disgust for all his past life, especially for his sexual misdeeds, that it seemed to him that all the fantasies that had been previously imprinted on his mind were now erased. Thus from that hour until August 1553, when this is being written, he never again gave the slightest consent to temptations against chastity. For this reason the vision may be considered the work of God, although he did not dare to claim it to be so.'

VANQUISHED BY GOD

This statement is a marvel of psychological insights, an example of discernment of spirits on the part of the one who would one day give precise rules for discerning spirits. Ignatius relates this episode very carefully, but he

'From experience he knew that some thoughts left him sad, while others made him happy.'

does not dare say with certainty that it came from God. On the other hand, he positively states the exceptional and lasting effects that resulted from it, and he was convinced that so radical a transformation could not have come about as a result of his own efforts or his natural inclinations. This was the moment in his life when he became a convert, a man in need of profound redemption, a man driven to find ways to make up for lost time. It was then, rather than at the fortress of Pamplona, that Ignatius fell, wounded and vanquished. The disgust he spoke of was not the cause of his transformation; rather, it was the effect of a light that had flooded him from within, enabling him to see the emptiness of the abyss that lay at his feet and, at the same time, marking out the pathway to the Absolute.

#10

How well do you read your inner experience of sadness and happiness?

11. A Change of Soul

SPIRITUAL GUIDE

At that very moment, Ignatius began to become another man. 'His brother and other members of the household recognised from his exterior the changes that had been working inwardly within his soul.' Was it possible that this change could have gone unnoticed by Doña Magdalena, his brother's wife, whom Ignatius described as a person 'who was ever sensitive to the marvels of God'? Ignatius began to see everything in a different light. He was now a person engrossed in thought. To the surprise of his family, he rediscovered his freedom, and a new kind of warm affection came into being within him. 'Without a care in the world, he persevered in his reading', just as he had done before, when he was absorbed in books about knight errantry. He followed out his good resolutions and spent time talking about the things of God with the members of the household. This was the supreme proof of the change that had taken place in him, especially when we recall that he had never before divulged anything to anyone about his interior emotional stirrings, not even to his brother, the priest. Now his words produced an effect because they were laden with something that came from within his own being. It was his first experience as a spiritual guide.

At this time, however, he still had a natural tendency toward harshness and excess. One instance suffices: Doña Magdalena had told a white lie and, when Ignatius heard about it, 'he rebuked her harshly and told her she could not sit at the same table with him, and for a few days he even gave her the silent treatment'.

WRITING

Ignatius got the idea of selecting from his chosen books the most important events in the life of Christ, and these he wrote down in a notebook, soon covering three hundred pages. The psychological effort involved in consigning to the written page favourite thoughts and sentences causes their meaning to sink into a person's soul and fixes them in their memory. Ignatius would later write in the introductory annotations to the *Spiritual Exercises*: 'It is not much knowledge that builds and satisfies the soul, but the intimate understanding and relish of the truth.' And so, on 'polished and lined paper', he wrote out the passages that had moved him and that he had savoured interiorly, the words of Christ in red ink and the words of Our Lady in blue. His precise and detailed account of what he had done at that time still has an unsophisticated freshness about it and does not at all conform to the image of the tough military man that some still insist on seeing in him. A simplicity so genuine and transparent could only have sprung from the fountain of an innocence rediscovered. Unamuno, with an intuition worth tons of erudition, gave us the key to this and Ignatius's other simple excesses when he said: 'The hero is always a child within; his heart is always the heart of a child; the hero is nothing more than a child become big.'

PRAYER

Ignatius also spent some of his time 'in prayer'. This is the first time we come across this phrase so fraught with mystery. It is not difficult for a person to pray when he finds his soul overflowing with desires and projects, when he is invaded by feelings of loathing for the life he has been leading, and when he has need of help. Ignatius would have used the prayer *Anima Christi (Soul of Christ)*, which is often incorrectly attributed to himself. We also know, thanks to a conversation he had years later with a Jesuit novice who was worried because of the affective attachment he bore for his family, that he had to hand a Book of Hours, which was costly and richly illustrated. Ignatius confided to the novice that in the early days of his conversion, he had found in a Book of Hours a picture of the Virgin Mary that bore a striking resemblance to his sister-in-law, Doña Magdalena. The face of the Virgin had troubled him by stirring up human affections in him, and so his solution was to cover the picture with a piece of paper. Only with the passage of time would he become more gentle with himself.

CONTEMPLATION

Each day, Ignatius's soul was becoming more pliant, more susceptible to the subtle influence of consolation. 'His greatest consolation was to gaze upon the heavens and the stars, which he did often and for long stretches of time, because when doing so he felt within himself a powerful urge to be serving our Lord.' By the end of his days, Ignatius, who had been so reticent when it came to expressing poetic feelings, would allow other fleeting outbursts of similar emotion to escape from his heart, such as the famous remark: 'How sordid is the earth when I contemplate the heavens!' On another occasion, he spoke about contemplating flowers. Ignatius was contemplating nature in a way he had never imagined he would. Like Francis of Assisi, whom he admired so much, he let himself be open to an invasion of cosmic feelings. But with him these sentiments were transformed into a dynamic force geared toward action. While he is considered the master of the art of will-power, his hidden secret was lodged in feelings, in the way he came 'to feel interiorly'. All his life he allowed himself to be governed by vague interior waves, which he called 'movements'. Methodically, he would seek out their meaning. He would later learn that there were periods of dryness bereft of all feelings, when affective love and love of service would have to depend solely on sheer will-power.

Ignatius began to see everything in a different light.

CARTHUSIAN

Would this quiet man who gazed intently on the heavens become a contemplative? Even though he was passionately attached to living the present moment in all of its riches and depth, he still considered the future and imagined what he would do after he returned from Jerusalem. 'He desired to be entirely well so that he could take to the road.' He was enthralled by the idea of living a life of perpetual penance, hidden away, eating only vegetables. He desired 'to indulge the hatred he had conceived against himself' and dreamt of entering the famous Carthusian monastery of Seville, 'without saying who he was so as to be held in scant esteem'. One day he surprised one of the servants, who was being sent on an errand to Burgos, by entrusting him with a secret commission to obtain information on the Rule followed by the Carthusians there. The man fulfilled his mission, and Ignatius was satisfied with the information he had brought him. But first he had to go to Jerusalem as he had promised, and soon, too.

How has the contemplative dimension grown within you?

12. Leaving Loyola, February 1522

BREAKING FAMILY TIES

In order to go to Jerusalem, Ignatius had to cut ties with his family, while keeping secret the project that was simmering in his heart. He probably left Loyola in February 1522. This breaking-away point had incalculable personal, familial and social consequences. Ignatius himself felt confident and free, but he was afraid of his family's reaction, and especially did he fear his brother Martín, who was his guardian and the head of the family.

For once, the intrepid Ignatius did not fight face to face; he sought some pretext to justify his leaving. He hinted to his brother that he thought it would be good if he went to Navarrete to see the Duke of Nájera, his former patron, who knew that he was now healed. But Martín was not caught off guard. 'He took Ignatius from one room to another and with many protestations of love begged him not to make a fool of himself, but to consider what hopes people had in him, and to see what he could make of himself, and similar other words, all with the purpose of turning him away from his good intentions.' His family wanted him to be as they were, which is reminiscent of Kierkegaard's delightful parable about the eaglet that is tamed by ducks. 'Ignatius answered in such a way that, without departing from the truth about which he was always very scrupulous, he avoided a direct issue with his brother.'

CONVERTED PASSION

Ignatius prepared for the journey as if he were going to settle in at the house of his protector, the Duke. He packed his bags, dressed in all his finery, and did not forget to attach his sword and dagger to his belt. A careful observer would have noticed something about the way he looked at people around him, because whoever says goodbye for an indefinite period of time, and possibly for ever, caresses with his eyes the faces and characteristics of those he loves. His will was now possessed by something stronger than itself. His converted passion had pointed him to a new direction in life. 'So, riding a mule', Ignatius left Loyola in February 1522. He had defiantly thrown himself into the Pamplona adventure mounted on a horse at full gallop; now, gently guiding his mule, he began a new adventure, a future that was less defined. Unforeseeable consequences hide themselves behind the small but deliberately chosen actions in our lives.

He set out accompanied by two house servants who were sent along by the family to guarantee that he would arrive at his destination. His brother Pedro, who would become the parish priest in Azpeitia, the town close to Loyola, was also part of the group. This man, Ignatius's companion in the excesses of 1515, had fathered a daughter a few months before this historic journey. For Ignatius, he was the closest and most tangible 'man of the Church' that he had known.

VIGIL AT ARANZAZU

The lay man, Ignatius, persuaded the priest that they should 'make a vigil at the Chapel of our Lady of Aranzazu'. And so they climbed up to the little hermitage that was hidden away in the steep crags. Ignatius made his prayer, gaining added strength for the road. Many years later, he would recall the benefits he had received from that vigil in the darkness that was broken only by the dawn. Afterward, they went down to the house of one of their sisters, and Pedro remained there. This sister, Magdalena, had let Ignatius stay in her house for a few days after he was wounded at Pamplona. Here the brothers bade goodbye to each other. These goodbyes solidified the distance that had grown between them and the cool hostility and unfriendliness on the part of Pedro. They would never see each other again. Pedro died in 1529 on the way home from one of his numerous trips to Rome, where he would go to argue his case against the Poor Clare nuns of his native town.

VOW OF CHASTITY

As a result of the generosity of heart that prompted his making a vigil at the shrine, Ignatius not only regained his strength, but he also began to lose that powerful drive he thought was always with him. Accordingly, it was probably at Aranzazu that he made a vow of chastity. Many years later, he acknowledged that such was the case. 'Since he was afraid of being overwhelmed in matters regarding chastity more than in any other area, he made a vow of chastity before Our Lady, to whom he had a special devotion, while he was still en route.' Laínez vouches for the efficacy of the gesture and of the sought-for protection when he says, 'Although up until then he had been attacked and conquered by unchastity, from that moment until the present time, Our Lord gave him the gift of chastity, and, as I believe, to a high degree of perfection.' So that his vow would not remain in the realm of beautiful rhetoric, 'from that day when he left his native land, he took the discipline [a small scourge] every night'.

Ignatius's converted passion had pointed him to a new direction in life.

DEBTS PAID

Ignatius went on toward Navarrete, probably because he did not want to be involved in telling a lie. It does not seem likely that he saw the Duke face to face there. But despite the fact that he had already resolved to give up all material possessions, he did request the salary that was owed him. At the time, the treasury was seriously strained, but the Duke said that 'even though he lacked money for all else, he would never be short of money for Loyola', and he was even ready to put Ignatius in charge of one of his better pieces of property 'in recognition of the reputation he had earned in the past'. Ignatius did not care about being an overseer of any property or person; what he wanted was to become the protagonist in his own uncertain adventure. He took the money, however, asking that part of it be paid to unspecified persons to whom he was still in debt; the other part was to be used to refurbish a statue of the Blessed Virgin.

ALONE

Ignatius dismissed the servants who had accompanied him, having confided in them his plan to go to Montserrat 'as a poor penitential pilgrim'. This was the last trace his family had of him for thirteen years, until he returned briefly to Loyola in 1535. Had he so desired it, he might once more have tasted the sweetness of high society and had doors opened for him to a promising future. But he followed his own lonesome path, a choice of his own making.

Ignatius goes /travels to Jerusalem

Recall decisive choices that you have made alone.

13. 'He set out alone riding his mule', Spring 1522

DOING MORE FOR GOD

Thirty years on, Ignatius described in his *Autobiography* his frame of mind as he jogged along on his mule: 'He had determined to practise great penances not so much with an idea of making satisfaction for his sins, as to make himself agreeable to God. Thus he was determined to do the same penances the saints had done, and even more. From such thinking he took all his consolation. He never took a spiritual view of anything, nor did he even know the meaning of humility, charity or patience, or that discretion was a rule and measure of these virtues. Without having any reason in mind, his sole idea was to perform these great external works, because the saints had done so for God's glory.'

THE MOOR AND THE MULE

'On the road there occurred an incident that is worth relating for the better understanding of how our Lord dwelt with his soul, which, although still blind, had a great desire to serve him in every way he knew.' A Moor caught up with him and 'they fell into talking, and the conversation turned on Our Lady. The Moor admitted that the Virgin had conceived without man's aid, but he could not believe that she had remained a virgin as a result of the birth process'. He explained the reasons for his thinking, and the theological arguments advanced by Ignatius did not make him change his mind. The Moor then took his leave and hurried on out of sight, 'leaving the pilgrim [Ignatius] with his own thoughts on what had taken place'.

Ignatius was caught up in a tide of emotion, moving from discontent to sorrow for failing in his duty, to wild indignation against the Moor for his audacity, to an urge to defend the honour of Our Lady, to the desire to search out the Moor, not merely to tie him captive to his mule and bring him to Our Lady of Montserrat where he would make him kneel at her feet, but with the intention of stabbing him a number of times with his dagger for what he had said. 'He struggled with this conflict of desires for a long time, uncertain to the end as to what he ought to do', because among other things, he would have to turn off from the royal highway to pursue the Moor.

Tired from indecision, he decided to let the mule go on with the reins slack so that it could make the decision. Despite the fact that the road taken by the

Moor toward the village was wider than the royal highway, Ignatius's mule chose the latter, thereby saving the Moor from possible death and Ignatius from the slave galleys. So he continued his way to Montserrat, thinking as always about the great deeds he was going to do for the love of God.

VIGIL OF ARMS
At this stage, despite his exercises in introspection at Loyola, Ignatius was no longer looking into his interior. He was confident that God asked him for generosity alone. He was thinking of imitating the penances of others, not about repentance for his own sins. Thoughts corresponding to the knightly adventures recounted in *Amadis of Gaul* came to his mind. He determined, therefore, on 'a vigil of arms through the whole night, without ever sitting or lying down, but standing a while and then kneeling a while before the altar of Our Lady, where he resolved to leave his fine attire and to clothe himself in the armour of Christ'. Such a ritual was already prescribed for knights in Spanish law. The knight who would make the vigil should be 'sometimes kneeling down and sometimes standing rigidly erect … for the knights' vigil of alms is not designed for amusement, nor for anything like that, but to beg God to protect them … as men who are entering a career of death'.

Ignatius arrived at Montserrat on 21 March 1522. It was the first stop in his pilgrimage. He had long dreamed of coming here because devotion to Our Lady of Montserrat was popular in the Loyola region. Our elegant knight arrived at the monastery 'with expensive, beautiful, and fine clothes … in the fashion and style of soldiers'. He decided to divest himself of all that he had, as a first step in his pilgrimage to Jerusalem. He had no difficulty arranging that his mule should be given to the Benedictine monastery. It was not unusual either that a friend should hang up before the altar of Our Lady of Montserrat the sword and dagger that the knight had entrusted to him in confidence. For many years, these arms remained on the grille where the statue of the Black Madonna is placed.

IN PILGRIM GARB
Hanging his fine clothes on the grille beside his arms would have wrecked the complete anonymity with which Ignatius wanted to proceed. So, with the following gesture, he annihilated his entire past: 'On the vigil of Our Lady's Annunciation, March 24, in the year 1522, he went at night, as secretly as he could, to a poor man and, removing his fine clothes, gave them to him and put on the attire he so wanted to wear.' In a large town near Montserrat, he had bought the clothes that he had decided to wear for the journey to Jerusalem. He remembered the purchase very distinctly as 'some cloth of the type used for making sacks, with a very loose weave and a rough prickly

surface'. Someone made him a long garment from it that went all the way down to his feet. He had also bought a staff as well as a small bowl, obligatory gear for a pilgrim, and finally a pair of sandals, but he did not use both of these. One of his legs was still bandaged and in bad shape, so much that it was swollen by the end of each day, even during those times when he rode. So he wore one sandal only, on the foot of this bad leg, and had thus arrived at Montserrat.

Ignatius decided to divest himself of all that he had.

THE RICH BEGGAR

To cast aside his finery meant more than embracing a life of poverty; it meant breaking away from whatever was symbolic of his standing in others' eyes. Ignatius, dressed in his pilgrim robe, was now disguised as a poor unknown – as if taking off his clothes would strip him of all realisation of who he was, who his family was, and what his name and reputation meant. There is something of the 'hippy' in this theatrical rupture with the past.

Vigil at Montserrat

What have you to let go of in order to be freer to serve God?

14. A Life-change, Montserrat, March 1522

CONFESSION

Before making his vigil of arms, 'he made a general confession in writing which lasted three days'. The confessor with whom he shared his jealously guarded intentions was Jean Chanon, a saintly French monk who also knew a thing or two about what it meant to give away wealth generously, for he had himself renounced the revenues from an ecclesiastical office. He was a competent man for understanding and guiding this newly arrived, intensely zealous pilgrim, whose confession was far from trivial or routine.

The prudent confessor realised that he was dealing with a penitent who was accustomed to acting out the books he had read and who was now disposed to re-evaluating his life. He may have given him either a book containing a compilation of sins that he often gave to pilgrims who knew how to read, or a copy of the monastery's treasured work, _Exercises of the Spiritual Life_ by Cisneros. This book emphasised the importance of methodical steps in the spiritual process, and was especially strong on the way in which the practice of prayer should be treated.

LEARNING METHOD IN PRAYER   _Discipline_

Ignatius knew well that one had to have a method when it came to breaking a horse, learning to play music, firing a crossbow and producing artistic penmanship. He was now about to learn that the road he had undertaken was not about extraordinary and disconnected exploits, but was made up of interior stages – purification, illumination and union – and that a general confession was not an end of the process but a beginning. He would learn that there were rules and precautions for how to examine one's conscience and control one's thoughts; that there were helps for learning how to pray, such as the invocation at the beginning of the prayer, the control of the imagination, and an ordered reflection by means of points for parts of the prayer; and that the colloquy or conversation with God develops spontaneously. It was not enough that he should know all about these things; it was necessary that he patiently exercise himself in them. This was a revelation, an authentic discovery that made a profound impression on him. The results of this insight made themselves evident in the notes he began to jot down, which he would afterward call _Spiritual Exercises_.

TOWARD MANRESA

Dressed in sackcloth, his new badge of knighthood, Ignatius had spent the night of 24 March 1522 in prayer before Our Lady's altar. Lost within the crowds of pilgrims and hidden by the friendly shadows of the church, he received Holy Communion. Then 'at daybreak he left to avoid being recognised'. He did not take the road to Barcelona, 'where he would meet many who would recognise and honour him'. Instead, he made a detour to a town that turned out to be Manresa, and there he decided to spend a few days in a hospice 'and to make a few notes in his book that he carried very carefully with him and that was a source of great consolation for him'. He had experienced too many things in too short a time and therefore he had a need to stop and pour out his emotions in writing on the pages of the only treasure he kept in his knapsack: his notebook.

THE INNOCENT BEGGAR

Without realising it, Ignatius had left a storm behind. All of his disguises and precautions were of no avail. Someone had followed him, caught up with him, recognised him as the owner of the clothes, and anxiously asked him if he had indeed given them to a poor man, as the beggar had asserted. The beggar had been in as much a hurry to pass himself off as a rich man as Ignatius had been to pass himself off as a poor man! Ignatius told the plain truth. He did not feel he had to say who he really was, where he had come from, nor what his family name was – not even to free the innocent beggar. 'I gave him the clothes,' Ignatius answered tersely, while 'tears of compassion started from his eyes'. He recorded in his *Autobiography* that 'he felt compassion for the poor man to whom he had given his clothes because he realised that the poor man was being harassed since they had presumed that he had stolen them'.

Thus in the first hour of his lonely anonymity and profound meditation, he had discovered a nameless neighbour caught up in the most grotesque and deplorable helplessness. He who was able to have his bones sawn off without uttering a whimper, doing nothing more than tightening his fists, now wept with compassion. Although his weeping was most probably at variance with the tenets of orthodox chivalry, it is nevertheless rich in significance for understanding the heart of Ignatius.

'THE PILGRIM'

Our pilgrim who has now made his way down from Montserrat wanted to be nothing more than a Christian, a real apprentice Christian. He was still impregnated by self-willed sanctity, for he was obsessed with notions of doing great things by his own decision, rather than enduring them or experiencing

Ignatius was determined to begin 'the adventure of a poor Christian'.

them. He wanted to achieve his sanctity by shortcuts. Without his being conscious of the fact, he was a 'chosen instrument', but he never suspected 'how much he had to suffer' (Acts 9:15-16). There were still many things for him to learn, but he was determined to begin 'the adventure of a poor Christian'. He wanted to be so poor that he would even renounce his own name. He would no longer be known to others as Iñigo but as Ignatius; much less would he be a Loyola. He would simply be a pilgrim, an anonymous Christian, a Christian without a proper name, but not without identity, not without Christian fervour. Throughout his *Autobiography,* he would refer to himself simply as 'the pilgrim'.

Revisit a moment when you made a fresh start in life. Does the memory of it give you energy?

15. Ignatius and Luther

THE WAR WITHIN

At this stage of his life, Ignatius took no part in the affairs of his family, of his country, of the papacy or of the wider political scene. The wars between Spain and France, the conquest of Mexico by Cortes, the return of the Basque Cano after circumnavigating the globe, the Muslim sacking of Belgrade and Rhodes – such events meant nothing to him except in so far as they might affect his travel plans for Jerusalem. He made no claims to the times in which he was living: they were not his. He was in the throes of a personal crisis and he had an insatiable thirst for the Absolute. The new editions of the Bible, the writings of Erasmus and Thomas More, passed him by. He was instead satisfied with his notebook containing his excerpts from *The Life of Christ* and *The Flower of the Saints*. He would deal with people of influence only to request a passport to the Holy Land.

LUTHER?

Not even Martin Luther was present in his world. Luther, condemned and ex-communicated in 1520, appeared before the Diet of Worms in April 1521, and was then walled up in Wartburg at the same time that Ignatius was recuperating from his wounds and re-evaluating his life at Loyola. He was responsible for the tremendous upheaval that was devastating the European world at the time when Ignatius began his pilgrimage. But the idea of himself being the antagonist to Luther, or the organiser of the anti-Protestant fighting forces throughout Europe, or of becoming the knight errant for the Catholic Reformation, had never crossed the mind of our anonymous pilgrim. He had made a vow of chastity freely and spontaneously at the very time when Luther was mocking the tyranny of religious vows, which he considered unnatural and contrary to the Gospel. He was simply Ignatius, an unknown pilgrim, whereas the name of Luther was resounding throughout Europe.

REFORM OF CHURCH OR SELF?

Luther was almost ten years older than Ignatius, and already well advanced along the road he had chosen to follow to the very end, whereas Ignatius was still beginning his journey, dressed in sackcloth and plodding along the road with one sandal on and one off. Luther attacked the Church head on, lashed out mercilessly against it, separated himself from it – all in the name of the Gospel. Ignatius did not go out to reform the Church; he sought to reform himself from within. He was a quiet man, the master of the soft, serious word whispered in the ear at the opportune time. He did not judge. It is possible that he did not even have time to think about the Church. He realised that everything could and should be good and that the bad comes from our misguided choices. For him, the Church was like a sheltering roof overhead, or a lap as snug as the lap of a mother, or like the air one breathes without asking at each moment whether it is polluted or not.

SIMILARITIES

There were similarities between the two men. Both Martin Luther and Ignatius were reclusive heroes; both were passionate, and each was seduced and conquered by an intense inner experience, the one in his monastery tower and the other in his Manresa cell. Their interior worlds were sufficiently seductive and obsessive to absorb all of their energies at every moment of the day and night. The personal experience of each had more power than any kind of theoretical knowledge, and it was from their experience that they hammered out their respective beliefs. Both had a certain sense of the poetic, a candour opposed to deceit, a generosity alien to any form of calculation. Each had had an experience of sin and of self-loathing that had shaken him to the core of his being, but this experience had rendered both of them more open to the long-awaited peace, the consolation that was the fruit of their convictions. At a particular time in his life, Ignatius would have understood very well these words of Luther: 'My rebellious flesh burns me with a devouring fire. I, who should be the prey of the spirit, am consumed by the flesh, by lust, sloth, idleness, torpor.' A French biographer of Luther observed that the solitary, lonely Luther did not so desperately stand in the need of teaching, 'but of a spiritual life, inner peace, liberating certainty, and rest in the Lord'. The same can be said of Ignatius.

FAITH AND WORKS

Each man transformed his way into a universal teaching, because both of them were convinced that it is in the heart of the human person, rather than in institutions, that the decisive battles are fought, and that human hearts, with their miseries and yearnings, are all alike.

Both Martin Luther and Ignatius would broadcast the discovery that brought them happiness; the one will raise a hue and cry with the assistance of the printing press; the other, in quiet corners, will meet face to face with his conversation partner. Both will be men of certitude. Self-confident and provocative, each of them will hurl out challenges; the one will defy Rome, the other will brave various inquisitional courts. Both are passionate Christians. Luther sees Christ as the Redeemer who gives us everything. Ignatius will not argue with this position, but he will see that Christ asks something more from us than faith alone: he asks us to follow, imitate and serve him so as to be able to offer him our will, even if it is a weak will.

If today Luther and Loyola were to take stock of their respective legacies, they might very well be able to ask themselves the same question: 'Have my work and my followers been faithful to my original generous designs, to that first love, so full of illusions and sincerity, that was my first real encounter with Christ?'

Both Ignatius and Martin Luther were convinced that it is in the heart that the decisive battles are fought.

#15

Criticism of the Church or self-reform: Where do you stand?

16. To Manresa, March 1522

THE POOR PILGRIM

An insecure life, an uncertain future, a life dependent on daily handouts: these would be Ignatius's routine after leaving Montserrat in March 1522. He had left in order to flee public notice. Possibly someone there had directed him to the hospice at Manresa, only a few hours away, where he would be able to spend a few days writing down the experiences he had been living through. At the same time, he would be making some headway on his journey toward Jerusalem. These 'few days' turned into eleven months, months that proved to be the crucial interlude that would leave an indelible mark on his life. Not only the sketchy outline of the little booklet that would become the *Spiritual Exercises* would see the light of day at Manresa; there are some who maintain that the germ of the Society of Jesus can be detected in his famous vision on the banks of the Cardoner River. For this reason, it is understandable why Jesuit historiography puts such importance on these two formative events, but it does so in hindsight. Let us simply follow along with Ignatius on his journey, keeping in mind that, ever since his adventure with the Moor, he refers to himself as 'the pilgrim', the name that will define perfectly his attitudes for a long time to come. The pilgrim is one who ventures into a foreign land, who makes himself an alien, who loses contact with the familiar props of his ordinary life, and who deprives himself of all help other than the charity that people show to those whom they do not know, but who have the indications of being poor. Our pilgrim is now going to see life from a point of view beyond all his previous experience, that is, through the eyes of a beggar. He will no longer think about life as a beautiful adventure, but he will live it to the ultimate limits of total self-renunciation. 'The greatest enemy to heroism', says Unamuno, 'is the shame of seeming to be poor.'

MANRESA

Manresa was a small industrial centre of a few thousand inhabitants whose lives were centred around cotton growing, manufacturing or trading. They were used to seeing pilgrims passing through their town on their way to and from Montserrat, but they had never seen the likes of him who now made his appearance among them. Ignatius was a young man, still strong and robust.

In one hand he carried a pilgrim's staff, and he was dressed in a garment of sackcloth that went down to his two feet, one of which was bare and the other was slipped into a flat sandal, made from esparto grass. He would have been carrying a knapsack filled with papers and writing materials, his inseparable book of hundreds of pages, and other items, one of which was the picture of Our Lady of Sorrows that he had brought from Loyola and would keep at his side for many years, until the day in Rome when he gave it to his nephew Antonio.

HOSPITALITY

When a widow named Inés Pascual was returning slowly to Manresa from a day's pilgrimage at Montserrat, accompanied by her children and three other widows, a poor man approached them. He was carrying a pilgrim's staff. 'He was not very tall; his complexion was pale and flesh pink; he had a handsome, grave face, and especially he had great modesty of the eyes … he was very tired and walked with a limp in his right leg.' He asked if there was a hospice nearby where he could lodge. The appearance of this pilgrim, who 'was balding a bit' and who spoke in Castilian, touched the heart of Inés. She told him that he could find the hospice he was looking for in Manresa, and she invited him to join her group. They walked along slowly to enable him to keep up with them, but they were unable to persuade him to ride the little donkey they had at their disposal. They arrived late in Manresa. Now, the Catalans have the reputation of being a people endowed with practical common sense, and the common sense of Inés warned her against wagging tongues, and so she did not come into town in the company of the pilgrim nor bring him home 'because she was a widow and the man had a handsome face and was young'. She sent him on ahead to the hospice of Santa Lucia with one of the widows who worked there, and she requested that they give him every consideration. She also promised that she herself would look after him from her own house. On the first night, she sent him a dinner of good broth and some chicken because 'he had been walking with pain', and on the following days she sent him more chicken and soup. Within a week, the pilgrim had attracted the attention of everyone.

'THE HOLY MAN'

Ignatius's gentility would have been noticed very quickly by the good people who had dealings with him. Witnesses who participated in Ignatius's beatification process more than forty years after his death offer valuable supplementary material to his own recollections in his *Autobiography*. We learn that the children of Manresa sometimes followed the pilgrim, calling him 'the holy man'. An old woman testified that she had kept the scissors

Within a week the pilgrim had attracted the attention of everyone.

which she had used to adjust the length of the pilgrim's sackcloth. It seems it was longer on one side than on the other. Such trivia came from men and women whose intuitive conviction told them that they had been in the presence of a saint. The summary of these impressions is that in a very short time the people of Manresa came to recognise 'the holy man' in the traveller whom they had at first called 'the sack man'.

Ignatius had wanted his change of clothes to be the external sign of a changed interior, a radical change of life, and this was certainly the way that those who saw him and heard him speak interpreted his action. 'But for as much as he avoided the esteem of others, he was not long in Manresa before people were saying great things about him, all because of what had happened at Montserrat. His reputation started to grow and the people were saying more than what was true about him, that he had given up a large inheritance, etc.' People are usually given to gossip, and so exaggerated speculations about who he was abounded in the town.

#16

What is your experience of personal poverty or of helping the poor?

To Manresa

17. Admiration and Slander

MYSTERIOUS

As Ignatius began his new life, he came to know the open-handed, good-natured people of the working-class town of Manresa. He slept little, and when he did it was always on the floor, and he spent his time in reflection and prayer. He girded a strong rope around his sackcloth robe, to which he attached a small dangling cord with knots of varying sizes. Dressed in this manner, he began to attract attention, chiefly because of his modesty of the eyes and his reserve. The seriousness of what he said impressed people. Here was a penitent covering up some intriguing mystery. Inés Pascual was won over by his virtues and patience and she treated him as her own son. Later on, another widow became responsible for his food and laundry. During his stay, which he had intended to be only a short period, but which extended from March 1522 to February 1523, the pilgrim was lodged in several hospitable Manresan homes.

DAILY ROUTINE

Gradually, the people got used to the pilgrim's way of doing things. Every day he begged for alms. He ate no meat and drank no wine, even when it was offered. But he did not fast on Sundays, and if he was offered a little wine on that day he would drink it. Each day he attended High Mass, during which he would read the Passion; in the evening he would attend sung Vespers and Compline, which he loved dearly because of the music. He spent hours in prayer, whether at a hermitage of Our Lady, or at the Dominican church, or the hospital chapel, or in a nearby cave that he discovered. He would also spend time praying before the roadside crosses and he would stop to pray whenever the Angelus bell rang. He relied on his Book of Hours and his rosary, as well as vocal prayers, for the source of some of his prayer. He visited the hospitals, where he bathed the sick. He confessed and went to Holy Communion weekly. He punished his body with the discipline and hair shirt, but otherwise paid absolutely no attention to its needs. 'And because he had been preoccupied with the care of his hair, which was according to the fashion of the day – and he did have nice hair – he decided to let it grow wild, without combing or cutting it, or covering it with anything during the day or night. And for the same reason he let his toe nails and finger nails grow because he had taken excessive care also of them.'

ILL-HEALTH

Thus Ignatius became an imitator of the great penitents of pious legends, but this regime brought it about that 'even though he was strong and had a solid constitution, his body was totally changed'. The Manresa people remembered him during this period as the pilgrim with the young, ruddy complexion, who was gradually transformed into a lean and haggard man. Ignatius ruined his health for ever with his excesses. We discover a trace of the hard lesson he learned from this in the kindness he showed the sick later on in life and in the concern he would have for the health of young Jesuit students. He used to say then that we render more service to God when we are in good health. But this observation came about at a wiser period of his life, when he saw things from a different point of view.

FOLLOWERS

The pilgrim ate what was given to him, when it was given to him, and where it was given to him. When invited to eat at someone's house, he spoke little and skilfully sidestepped questions from the curious who wanted to know who he was. He was a sinner, period. He suppressed his naturally fiery temperament and answered questions with studied composure. He would speak with the children in the streets, to people who were solicitous of the needs of pilgrims, and to old people who wanted to hear what he had to tell them. His message was simple: one should not sin; one should examine one's conscience and make an effort to do better; it is good to confess and receive communion weekly.

Ignatius message

The pilgrim's measured and honest speech appealed to women, who were receptive to what he had to say. He began to have some faithful followers, 'honest women, married or widows'. These 'followed him religiously day and night, eager to hear what he had to say and to partake in the spiritual conversations he always offered, and were willing to assist him in the good works he did, either at the hospice or when he went to serve the sick, to wash their hands and feet, or when he busied himself with other poor people or orphans that were in the city. He would go out begging from door to door for them, and then, at set times during the day, he would distribute alms to them in a discreet manner by setting what he had collected before the door of the house where he was staying'.

BACKBITERS

Manresa, however, was, according to a witness, 'a very small town whose inhabitants were backbiters'. So there were those with evil and envious tongues who publicly spoke ill of the pilgrim, of what he was doing and of those who were associated with him. Since he was young, there was no lack of people who criticised him for being a bum. Others challenged him on what his family would now say of him, but he was not deflected. He depended totally on others for alms and he had no roof to shelter him, other than that which charity alone provided. He lived like a hermit, and, although he lived in proximity to others, his lifestyle was not in tune with theirs. He cared for the sick at the tiny hospice and for the poor who accepted his paltry handouts, and he treated them with the respect he had previously reserved for the nobility at Arévalo. He may well have returned on occasion to Montserrat to meet with the monk who had befriended him on his first arrival. He would have lived near the monastery, and would have given an account of how he was putting into practice the spiritual exercises he had been taught.

There was no lack of people who criticised Ignatius for being a bum.

How do you respond to admiration and to slander?

18. Doubts and Scruples

FROM JOY TO CONFUSION

Ignatius's early days at Manresa were filled 'with great and constant joy', according to himself. But then a disturbing thought began to insinuate itself, as if someone were saying deep within his soul: 'How can you stand a life like this for the seventy years you have yet to live?' Sensing that it was from the evil spirit, he answered interiorly with great vehemence, 'Wretch, can you promise me an hour of life?' So he overcame the temptation and peace returned to him. But then further confusion followed. 'Sometimes he felt so out of sorts that he found no relish in any of the prayers he recited, not even in hearing Mass.' Then again the lost joy would return, and sadness and desolation were removed 'just as when one snatches a cloak from another's shoulders'. The pilgrim was taken aback by these changes and asked himself: 'What kind of a new life are we beginning?' He stuck with his religious practices, however, and occasionally received words of comfort, like those of a pious old Manresan lady who told him she wished that Jesus Christ would appear to him some day.

SCRUPLES

Next, 'he had much to suffer from scruples'. In other words, having faced the crisis of what the future would bring, he now had to face the crisis of the past. On the advice of a reliable spiritual man, the pilgrim wrote down all that he was able to remember, and then read it off in confession. But it was to no avail because his scruples returned 'even with regard to minute and small matters'. Another confessor told him that he was not to confess anything more from his past life 'unless it was something absolutely clear'. But like all scrupulous people, the pilgrim 'considered everything was manifestly clear. And so the order benefited him not at all, and thus he continued in his anxiety'. His torment went on for months. In one of those extreme situations, in the solitude of his small room, 'he began to call out to God in a loud voice'. At this juncture in the *Autobiography*, he abandons the use of the third person and inserts the words of his heart-rending prayer: 'Help me, O Lord, since I find no help from people or from any creature. No trial would be too great for me to bear, if I thought there was any hope of finding that help. Show me, O Lord, where I may find it, and even though I should have to follow a little dog to help me, I would do so.'

SUICIDE?

Heaven did not answer this prayer, and a temptation arose, urging him to commit suicide by throwing himself into a deep hole that was close to his room. His strong ego dictated that it would be a sin to kill himself, and so the pilgrim repressed these temptations by crying out anew, 'Lord, I will do nothing to offend you.' He was now a prey to confusion, knowing the abyss of what it means to be human, deprived of moorings, and finding no relief from anyone or anything. For a whole week, this pilgrim with a will of iron refrained from eating or drinking anything, in imitation of the saint he had read about who would not eat or drink anything until God gave him the grace he had been seeking. His confessor advised him to desist, and he obeyed. For two days he was free from scruples, but on the third day while at prayer the remembrance of his past sins returned. This agony led to a disgust for the new life he had undertaken and a desire to give it all up.

LIBERATION

It was at this very moment that he realised that he was not holding the reins of his life in his own hand, that he could not place confidence in himself. It was then that an unexpected and hoped-for change took place; it was as if he had awakened from a bad dream. It was something akin to the 'hour' that psychoanalysts speak about. As he recalled what he had learned through experience about different spirits while he was at Loyola, he saw the knot in the tangle and discovered the key to the puzzle. Then, everything fell into place: he had found again his sanity and security. 'He therefore made a decision with great clarity of mind that he would not confess any of his past sins anymore. As a result of this resolution, his scruples disappeared immediately and he firmly believed that God's mercy had freed him.' He had rediscovered the basic confidence to live and the proper strategies to confront difficulties.

SCHOOLMASTER AND CHILD

So it was that the trials that came one after another during the first four months of his stay in Manresa finally gave way to a period of lightness of spirit that began around the month of August, 1522. This dawn that followed the blackest of nights throws into relief his solitude, his spiritual immaturity, and, above all else, it focuses on the beginnings of his new course of training by God. In his own account, 'God treated him at this time just like a schoolmaster treats a child he is teaching. Whether this was because of his

God treated Ignatius just like a schoolmaster treats a child.

thick and dull understanding or because he had no one to teach him or because of the strong desire God had given him to serve Him, he had always believed that God treated him in this way.'

How do you think God finds the task of teaching you?

19. On the Banks of the Cardoner, 1522

NEW MEANINGS

When Ignatius says that God was his schoolmaster, he does not mean, as Luther did, that he was radically liberated from the mediation of the Church. Just the opposite: he participated in the sacraments, immersed himself in traditional devotions, and took his problems to his confessor, whose direction he blindly obeyed. At the same time, he clearly understood that apart from all of these matters, God and God alone was teaching him as a schoolmaster teaches a young boy. This pupil that he was illuminating now seemed to see new meaning in the old truths he had learned from the study of his catechism, or that he had heard while he was sitting around the kitchen table at Loyola, or what he had subsequently picked up from the books he had read. With awe and wonder, he learned the unfathomable depths of things about which we speak today in terms that have been all but worn out by overuse: God, the Trinity, the creation and essence of creatures, the Eucharist, and the close presence of the humanity of Christ.

ENLIGHTENMENT

Ignatius had difficulty in articulating all of this, but what he did learn he describes in a delightful way. He also remembers the place where this enlightenment occurred: 'It seemed to be on the steps of the monastery, during the elevation at Mass.' But when it came to describing the experience itself, the task became much more difficult – the elevation of his spirit, seeing with the inner eye of the soul, and visual but non-audible images, were all accompanied by great joy and consolation and followed by much sobbing and uncontrollable tears. What God impressed upon his soul we do not know, but God branded him with a red-hot iron, because after these visions had ceased, their effects lasted. For the rest of his life, for instance, he felt great devotion while praying to the Holy Trinity. 'All these things he saw strengthened him at the time and always gave him such conviction that if there were no Scriptures to teach us in these matters of the faith, he would be resolved to die for them, merely because of what he had seen.' What a pity it is that the book he began to write on the Trinity has been lost. It consisted of more than eighty pages, and would certainly have been written in a devotional rather than an academic style.

ALL SEEMED NEW

Along the banks of the Cardoner River, there occurred the greatest of his experiences. 'Once he was going, out of devotion, to a church about a mile from Manresa. The road ran close to the river. As he went along, occupied with his devotions, he sat down for a moment facing the river that ran deep at that place. As he sat, the eyes of his understanding began to open and, although he saw no vision, he did see and understand many things, both spiritual things and matters of faith and learning. This took place with so great an enlightenment that everything seemed altogether new to him. This clarity was so great that in the whole course of his life, right up to his sixty-second year, even if he were to gather all the help he had received from God and all the many things he knew, and added them altogether, he does not think that they would equal all that he received at that one time. And thus, his understanding became enlightened in so great a manner that it seemed to him that he was a different man and that he had a different intellect from the one he had had before.'

A DIFFERENT MAN

Scientists of the soul refer to this transition from the rational, reflective consciousness to the field of profound intuition as 'an altered state of consciousness'. Such unexpected and indescribable experiences as the pilgrim underwent are special gifts given to privileged persons of very different religious backgrounds and in every era of history. They are not permanent states, but passing stages. Their effects, however, are stable and long-lasting. Peace and harmony take possession of such persons. What one has learned through discursive knowledge seems obscure and incomplete, compared to what comes through intuition. This illumination affects the deepest layers of one's being. The recipient becomes aware of the newness of things. From the depth of his interior, he communicates with the universe and with Someone who remains outside it, but who yet remains present to him in all of his difficulties. 'Everything seemed altogether new to him' and he had the impression of being 'a different man'. He began to see 'with other eyes than those that he had'. *A different man, other eyes, altogether new things* – these are charismatic phrases.

A GIFT TO SHARE

Illuminations such as the one Ignatius experienced are never an end in themselves. They are usually the point of departure for a person's insertion into the real world. Ignatius felt himself freer, more the creator of his self-identity, open to others in a different way. He gives up his excessive ways, trims his hair, pares his nails and abandons the idea of becoming a Carthusian because he sees 'the good effects he could have on souls through his dealings with them'. He wants to give to others what he has found. An extraordinary change has come about, transforming the recluse into an apostle. Ignatius had gained over the years considerable personal experience about the problems of the human heart, and how heavenly visitations, obstacles, deceits and discernments affected it. He gained insight into the ways of human freedom and he learned about 'the giant call', the term used by the German poet Rilke, the call to which the saints listen and respond. Ignatius believed that this 'giant call' was not a rare and reserved privilege and that the obstacles that prevented one from hearing it were not unusual either. From his Manresa days onward, he began to guide others along the path he had already travelled, in the 'conquest of self and the regulation of life in such a way that no decision is made under the influence of any inordinate attachment', as the *Spiritual Exercises* puts it.

Everything seemed altogether new to him.

Enlightened at the Cardoner

Do you sometimes see things in a new way?

20. Barcelona, 1523

CHICKEN SOUP

During his final months in Manresa, Ignatius was eager 'to help other people who came looking for him to discuss the affairs of their souls' and he used to give lectures in the little chapel of Santa Lucia to the devout women who liked to hear him. But he became ill on a number of occasions. Once, for a whole week, he remained in a state of complete prostration, which gravely concerned the families who cared for him. Inés Pascual blamed her own negligence for this mysterious sickness and she set out to cure it with her infallible remedy for all ailments – chicken soup! That winter of 1522 was exceptionally cold, and the solicitous women were successful in their efforts to make Ignatius dress properly. He put on shoes and covered his head 'with a large bonnet of very coarse cloth shaped like a little beret'.

LEAVING MANRESA

'The time he had set for his departure to Jerusalem was drawing near. So, at the beginning of the year 1523, he left for Barcelona in order to set sail.' His time spent in Manresa was not lost. Later, he would designate this period in his life as his 'primitive church' phase. Never would he forget the good people of Manresa who gave him food and lodging. The town kept remembrances of its own: his sackcloth gown and his belt were regarded as relics. Many places became stamped by the memory of his presence. Without knowing who he had been, people followed him because they knew what he had become. The ever-kind Inés provided the pilgrim with a tiny room in Barcelona. He was a guest who caused no inconvenience. He had a place where he could sleep and pray. That was all he needed, because he followed the same daily schedule in Barcelona that he had in Manresa.

GOD ALONE

Ignatius's main goal in Barcelona was to book a passage on a ship bound for Rome, not a very difficult thing to do. But over and above this, he wanted free passage and he wanted to go alone. On this adventure, he would give up all human security and would live totally dependent on God's providence. Many people who held him in high regard argued with him that it was only reasonable that he team up with someone on this trip because, among other things, he spoke neither Italian nor Latin. But he said that he would not accept any company or protection, because 'his whole purpose was to have God alone for refuge'. 'He wanted to exercise the virtues of charity, faith and hope. If he had a companion, he would expect help from him when he was hungry, and if he should fall down, he would expect him to help him get up and he would also confide in him and on this account would feel affection for him.' What he said came right from his heart. It was with such a disposition that he wanted to set sail, not merely all by himself, but also with no provisions for the journey.

'A GOOD-FOR-NOTHING!'

The ship's master gave Ignatius free passage, but forbade him to embark unless he had the prescribed amount of ship's biscuit to last him for the journey. This posed a problem of conscience for Ignatius, and he began to ask himself, 'Is this the hope and faith you have in God who would not fail you?' He brought his dilemma to a confessor, who recommended that he take a middle course. He would embark with the biscuit, but to get it he would have to beg for it. And so he began to beg. One woman lectured him on the point as follows: 'You certainly seem to me an evil man, going around this way as you do. You would do better to go back to your own home, instead of wandering around the world like a good-for-nothing.' The pilgrim accepted the reproach calmly and humbly and he agreed that he was a good-for-nothing and a sinner. Struck by this answer, the good woman gave the pilgrim bread, wine and other items for his voyage. Another asked him: 'Where are you sailing?' He answered with a half-truth and said he was going to Rome. 'So,' said she, 'you want to go to Rome, do you? Well there is no telling how those who go there come back.' This spirited Barcelona woman did not have a high opinion of the renaissance Rome of Pope Leo X. Along with such unsolicited exhortations and lectures, the pilgrim managed also to collect his provisions. In fact, he even counted a surplus of six coins that he scrupulously left behind on a waterfront bench.

SPIRITUAL PERSONS

While waiting for his ship to sail, the pilgrim sought out 'spiritual persons', as he called them, persons who could understand his interior state. But only one found favour in his eyes. This was an old Manresan woman who was nameless and who asked God that Jesus might appear to Ignatius. She was 'a woman of many years, who for a long time had been a servant of God. She was known as such in many parts of Spain, so much so that the Catholic King had called her once to seek her advice'. Ignatius noted that 'she was the only one who seemed to be deeply versed in the spiritual life'. As time passed, he

Ignatius wanted to undertake this adventure by giving up all human security.

became more mature, less dependent, and given to greater solitude. 'After leaving Barcelona, he lost for good this eagerness to seek out spiritual persons.'

How deeply do you try to depend on God's providence?

21. Rome and Venice, 1523

AN ANGRY IGNATIUS

Ignatius crossed from Barcelona to Gaeta in Italy in five days, thanks to a strong following wind. When the passengers disembarked, about 20 March 1523, the plague was ravaging Italy. The pilgrim set out immediately on foot for Rome. He was joined by a young man and a mother accompanied by her daughter, who was dressed as a boy. All of them begged along the way. The trek was long and not without frightening moments. They had intended to spend the first night in an inn, near which there were many soldiers huddled around a large fire. The soldiers gave them food to eat and were particularly generous in sharing their wine with the newcomers, 'as though they wanted to warm them up', commented the pilgrim, who knew very well the ways of soldiers.

Afterward, the travellers divided into pairs, the two women retiring to a room and the pilgrim and the young man to the stable. About midnight, Ignatius was awakened by the shouts of the woman and her daughter, who, by the time he got to the inn, were already in the courtyard weeping and saying the soldiers had attempted to rape them. For a few moments, the former bold and valiant soldier came to life again in the humble pilgrim. So angry did he become and so loud did he shout that all the people in the house were frightened and the soldiers gave up what they had intended to do. The young man had vanished under the protection of the darkness, but the two women and the pilgrim continued their journey even though it was still night.

PLAGUE

They arrived at Fondi, but the gates of the town were closed, so they had to sleep in a church. But even during the day, they were not allowed to enter the city because of sanitary precautions, and outside the city they were not successful in collecting alms. They went to a nearby castle, but the exhausted pilgrim, already weakened by the hardships of a sea journey, could go no further. The mother and daughter continued their trip toward Rome. As fortune would have it, on that very day crowds of people came out of the city to receive the noble lady to whom the town belonged. In a gesture of desperation, the pilgrim literally planted himself in the middle of the road so that they would not take him for a victim of the plague because of his drawn face, but would say 'he was ill only from weakness' and was asking the favour to enter the town. Once inside, he collected a good number of small coins, recovered his health and arrived in Rome on Palm Sunday, 29 March 1523.

ROME

Ignatius spent Holy Week in Rome in prayer and in begging alms. He received the blessing of Adrian VI and the required pontifical permission to go to the Holy Land. Someone had written out for him, in Latin, the form petitioning the licence, which has since been found in the Vatican archives. Again he was assured that without money it would be absolutely impossible for him to book a passage from Venice to Jerusalem. But nothing could change his mind, because 'in his soul he had great certainty, which would admit of no doubt, that he would find some way of getting to Jerusalem'.

TO VENICE

About 13 April 1523, Ignatius took the road to Venice with six or seven gold coins that he had been given to defray his passage. He had accepted this money 'because of the fear with which others had inspired him of not being able to get to Jerusalem otherwise'. Two days after he left Rome, he repented of his lack of confidence by taking the money, and so he determined to use it as alms for the poor. The trip, which was made all the way on foot, was rich in misfortune and hardships. His itinerary, through a succession of Italian towns, would today be considered an ideal tour of the back roads of Italy, but at the time it was made difficult because of the plague. He ate as he could and slept under porticoes or in the open fields. One morning, a man who had spent the night near him, fled when he saw Ignatius's sallow, drawn face, since he thought for certain that he was looking at a man stricken by the plague. Such was our pilgrim 'of the sorry countenance'.

A VISION OF CHRIST

Getting into Venice presented more problems. Some of his fellow pilgrims went off to get a health certificate at Padua. He could not keep up with them because they walked too fast, and so they left him behind 'at nightfall in a vast field'. It was one of his worst experiences of total abandonment, but he tells us that here 'Christ appeared to him in his usual way', referring to his Manresa days. This vision consoled him, gave him strength and helped him to arrive in Padua, where he went in and out of the city without having to show a health certificate, much to the amazement of his more prudent fellow travellers. Then, still without the required certificate, he came to Venice. The guards inspected everyone who had arrived, allowing only him to enter the city of the canals undisturbed. It was mid-May; he still had two months to wait for passage to the Holy Land.

UNEXPECTED HELP

Ignatius supported himself by begging and he slept in the Piazza di San Marco. One day, he met a rich Spaniard living in Venice who asked him what he was doing there and where he was going. This man invited him to come and eat in his house and gave him a few days' lodging. At first, the pilgrim remained silent at the table, listening, eating and answering the questions he was asked, and then at the end of the meal, picking up bits and pieces of the table talk, he began to speak about God. The family of this unexpected host became fond of him and persuaded him to remain with them. What was more, this unknown Spanish gentleman was successful in getting him a private audience with the Doge of Venice. The end result was that the Doge ordered that he be given passage aboard a ship that was taking the Venetian governor to Cyprus.

The trip, which was made all the way on foot, was rich in misfortune and hardships.

How do you cope with misfortune and hardships?

22. Jerusalem, September 1523

TO CYPRUS

A few days before the ship's departure from Venice to Cyprus, Ignatius was stricken with bouts of fever. The treatment he received was inadequate and on the very day of his departure he was given a purge. The doctor said that he could set sail, but only if his intention was to be buried en route. Ignatius, stubborn Basque that he was, boarded the ship, and after a period of continuous vomiting he began to feel better. The ship, going at a snail's pace because of the all-pervasive calm, took a whole month to arrive at Cyprus, where it finally touched shore on 14 August. All of this inactivity had fostered vice on board. The pilgrim chanced to see 'some individuals engaged in openly lewd and obscene behaviour', that is to say, homosexual activity. Ignatius severely reproved the guilty individuals. The three other Spaniards aboard pleaded with him not to overreact, because the crew were talking about dropping him off on some island. Soon after, however, they arrived at Famagusta in Cyprus. At the port of Larnaca, Ignatius embarked on another ship, with nothing more for sustenance than his hope in God. As a compensation, he had the vision of the nearness of Christ in the form of 'a large round object, as though it were of gold', and this brought him consolation and courage. On 19 August 1523, twenty-one pilgrims set sail from Cyprus and landed in Jaffa on the 31st. There they sang the *Te Deum* and the *Salve Regina*. Then, accompanied by members of the Franciscan Order, which had the jurisdiction of pilgrims, and by an escort of Turkish troops to secure their safety in this closed, hostile Muslim world, they mounted small donkeys and made their way toward Jerusalem.

THE HOLY CITY

As the pilgrims approached Jerusalem, one of the Spaniards among them announced that they were approaching the hill from where they would be able to see the Holy City for the first time. He recommended that all of them prepare their consciences for this event in silence. Just before arriving at the viewing spot, they came upon a number of Franciscans, one of whom was holding a cross on high. These had come from Jerusalem to welcome them. The pilgrims dismounted and proceeded on foot. 'When the pilgrim saw the city, he experienced great consolation, and all the others affirmed that they experienced the same and confessed that they felt a joy that did not seem natural.' The pilgrim was overcome by an awe and fervour that never left him during all the time he visited the holy places. The group visited all the holy places in Jerusalem, and then left under the escort of Turkish soldiers for Jericho, and there they saw the Jordan River. Their last two days were spent in the Jerusalem hostel of Saint John.

SEEING WITH THE IMAGINATION

Ignatius's eyes drank in the landscape, and what he saw was engraved for ever on his memory. Later, in the *Spiritual Exercises,* he would give a direction about the 'composition of place', that is, about having the retreatants place themselves imaginatively in the actual place where the mystery unfolds. After the eyes have seen, the imagination does its work, and the spirit follows along the footsteps of Christ into those places hallowed by him. Ignatius's powerful sense of Christ found a particular spiritual nourishment in the very concrete setting where Jesus' voice resounded and where he worked out our redemption. This longed-for Jerusalem pilgrimage meant more for Ignatius than performing a series of penitential devotions. It was an effort to grasp Christ, who, although no longer present in physical form in the places associated with his historical presence, became more ardently experienced each day within the heart of the pilgrim.

FORBIDDEN TO STAY

Ignatius desired with all his heart to remain for the rest of his days in these holy places; moreover, he secretly believed that his presence there could bring some help to others. He had brought Spanish letters of recommendation to this effect to the Father Guardian of the Franciscans, indicating that he wanted to remain in Jerusalem. But any missionary activity was all but impossible in this Muslim world. Even his plan to stay on in the Holy Land was impractical. The Franciscan House in Jerusalem was extremely poor and the fathers there had even considered sending some of their own members back on the pilgrim ship. The pilgrim, however, asked only that he might come to them occasionally to make his confession.

On the evening before the group's departure, the Franciscan Guardian dashed all his hopes. A man of great experience, he judged that Ignatius's project was preposterous. Others who had tried to lead the type of life that he was proposing ended up either in prison or dead. Ignatius argued that he would assume responsibility for his own fate, but the Franciscan Provincial made him understand that he himself had the exclusive jurisdiction over those who came to Jerusalem and that he could excommunicate anyone who refused to obey him. The pilgrim quietly accepted this painful decision.

What Ignatius saw in the Holy Land was engraved for ever on his memory.

WHITHER NOW?

To utilise his few remaining hours, he returned once again to the Mount of Olives to verify the direction of the feet in the stone believed to be imprinted with Christ's footprint at the moment of his ascension. Without a word and without even taking a guide, he slipped away from the others and went up to the place alone. He bribed the guards by giving them a pair of scissors. Shortly afterward, the alarm spread throughout the hospice that he had disappeared. One of the servants went out to look for him and found him on the road. The servant was very angry, threatened him with a huge stick, grabbed him violently by the arm and brought him back to the hospice as if he were a criminal. During this event, the pilgrim felt the help and nearness of Christ in a most tangible way.

Finally, after an unforgettable stay of twenty days, the pilgrim left Jerusalem on the night of 23 September. He had fulfilled the greatest desire of his life, and he considered all of the inconveniences he had suffered worthwhile. For the moment, he had to give up the idea of living and dying in Palestine, accepting this as a manifestation of God's will for him. His destiny was not to be found in Jerusalem as of now. Where, then, was it to be?

Does it help you to use your imagination in reading the Gospel scenes?

23. The Middle-aged Student, 1524

BACK TO VENICE

The pilgrim began his return home from Jaffa. After arriving in Cyprus, the group of pilgrims parted company and continued on home in three different ships. Some of the pilgrims asked a rich Venetian, the owner of the largest and best-equipped ship, to allow their penniless companion to make the journey with them, free of charge. The Venetian was deaf to their entreaties and even joked with them about their request. 'If this man is really a saint,' he said, 'let him cross the sea miraculously as Saint James did.' Ignatius ended up sailing in the smallest of the three ships. The two larger ones sank in a surprise storm. The third had a hard time of it, but it alone managed to reach Italy, landing at Apulia. The pilgrim had to face this bad weather in his miserable, shabby clothes, which consisted of a black jacket cut off at the shoulders, a pair of shorts made of coarse cloth that went as far as the knees, a pair of shoes and a short threadbare coat. Dressed in this fashion, he arrived in Venice in mid-January 1524 after two months at sea. At Venice, someone who had shown him hospitality on his way to Jerusalem gave him alms and a piece of cloth, which he folded several times over and placed on his stomach to protect himself from the intense cold.

STUDY

Despite so many months of wandering, Ignatius's future was still altogether uncertain and 'he kept thinking of what he ought to be doing'. His earlier plan to enter the Carthusians had gone by the board, having been supplanted by the desire, emerging from his Manresa experience, to help people. 'He finally felt more inclined to spend some time in studies', and thought again of Barcelona. We will never know anything about the long and involved interior process that led him finally to opt for this unexpected option. He was already thirty-three years old. He began his return trip to Spain by the land route, walking and begging all the way. At Ferrara, he gave a coin to a poor man, another of greater value to a second beggar, and to a third a coin of even greater value. Word soon spread and poor people came in droves. When he had given away everything, he asked pardon of the latecomers 'because he had nothing left to give'. From that day on, he had to beg for his food. No wonder that poor people cried out 'The saint! The saint!' whenever this bizarre-looking pilgrim walked out of the church.

ARRESTED

During his trek from Ferrara to Genoa in January 1524, Ignatius encountered some Spanish soldiers, who put him up for the night. Astonished that he had 'walked that road because it passed almost in the middle of the French and Spanish armies', they urged him to take a safer road, but he ignored their advice. Night was coming on and he had had nothing to eat all day. He came to a walled town, where the guards seized him and, taking him for a spy, 'they began to interrogate him, as they usually do with suspects'. He answered all their questions, saying that he knew nothing. They stripped him, inspecting his shoes and every part of his body to see if he was carrying any written messages. Finding nothing, they bound him and took him to their captain, who, they said, 'would make him talk'. He was dressed only in his shorts and jacket; they did not even let him put on his short cloak. As he was being led through the streets, he remembered how it must have been when Christ was arrested, and, thanks to this thought, he was able to walk fearlessly and courageously, with joy and elation. He was led to the palace, where the guards locked him in a downstairs room. A short time later, the captain made his appearance. The pilgrim deliberately gave him no sign of courtesy, responding to his questions with few words and long pauses. The furious captain thought he was deranged and he mocked him in front of his subordinate, saying, 'This fellow has no brains. Give him his things and throw him out.' Leaving the palace, he fell in with a Spaniard who lived in the town; he brought him home and gave him his first meal of the day and all that he needed for the night.

TO BARCELONA

Ignatius left the next morning and walked until late afternoon. Then two French soldiers spotted him and brought him to their captain, who turned out to be a Basque himself, and who ordered that the pilgrim be fed and treated well. Ignatius went on his way to Genoa and found a vessel bound for Barcelona, where he arrived with no other provisions than his hope in God. There was a great deal of the Franciscan bohemian spirit in his incredible undertaking, born out of stubbornness and pure hope. This last factor explains why the detailed and selected accounts of his adventures are unlike a tourist's journal, and indeed unlike even the diary of a pious pilgrim. Ignatius's account is a simple hymn to the providence that guided his steps.

DISTRACTIONS AT STUDY

Ignatius found a teacher in Barcelona who volunteered to teach him free of charge. Isabel Roser, a lady of Barcelona, promised to take care of his needs. Our superannuated student stood out as being very singular, not only because of his age, but because he had problems with concentration. His attention would be drawn away from study by delightful insights into spiritual matters. He mulled over this and was struck by the fact that these delights were a temptation, since they never came to him when he was attending Mass or praying. Thereupon he promised his master that 'as long as I can find bread and water in Barcelona to support myself, I will never miss any of your classes during the next two years'. Since he made this promise with great determination, he never again had those temptations. Taking the opposite of any compromise is a recurring theme in the life of Ignatius. He remained a man of prayer, who attended Mass regularly and who lived an austere life of poverty. He bored holes in his shoes and, by the time the winter of 1525 arrived, these holes had widened to the extent that nothing remained of the shoes except the upper parts.

Ignatius kept thinking of what he ought to be doing.

Arrested as a spy

Do you give time to thinking about what you ought to be doing?

81

24. Student in Barcelona, 1524-25

PRAYING AND BEGGING

In Barcelona, Inés Pascual welcomed Ignatius once again into her home, where he had spent three weeks prior to his departure for Jerusalem. She was described as 'a woman who loved the truth and would not tell a lie for all the gold in the world'. During the ravages of the plague, she had sheltered a lost child, and this young boy remembered the upstairs room that the pilgrim occupied in the little house; he recalled the wooden bed that had no mattress, and how Ignatius would spend hours on his knees in prayer. He said that Ignatius was a silent man, unwilling to converse, who spoke only when he was asked a question, but what he said 'would speak to the heart'. He attested that Ignatius came back from his pilgrimage to Jerusalem dressed in the same clothes he was wearing when he departed, and that he carried with him a rosary, which he said continuously.

Ignatius begged for his food during the whole time that he remained under Inés Pascual's roof. For him, the benefits that resulted from begging were an encounter with the unknown, the unpredictable; the experience of depending on pure charity that gives without question to a nameless poor person; the frequent scorn and the accompanying condescending lecture; and finally, the feeling of total hopelessness before people, along with a complete reliance and hope in God alone.

MOTHERLY CARE

Each week, one of the Barcelona ladies brought Ignatius a supply of flour, which Inés would knead and bake for him. Whatever he had not eaten, he would then distribute to the poor. It seems, too, that Ignatius used to bring home scraps of bread, eat the most unsavoury pieces and give away the best. On one occasion, the boys of the household looked through his knapsack and said, 'You've got a lot of bread down there.' The pilgrim answered gently, 'Help yourselves to it.' In spite of the disapproval of Inés, the boys accepted the invitation. 'You rascals, you should let him eat it!' she had said. The pilgrim intervened in this dispute and, in a most gentle way, said: 'Mother Pascual, let them alone; it gives me joy just watching them eat it all.' We may note here that perhaps the only woman in this world whom Ignatius called mother was Inés Pascual.

Inés's son, Juan, shared an upstairs room with the pilgrim. When the time came for them to retire, Ignatius would say to the young man, 'John, you go to bed now, I have something else I want to do.' The boy would get into bed and pretend that he was asleep, but in fact he would stay awake, fascinated, watching his roommate praying on his knees for hours on end and sighing aloud, 'My God, if only people knew you!'

BEATEN AND PAMPERED

The local Dominican nuns had the reputation of socialising with lay people. Ignatius visited them on a number of occasions and succeeded in convincing them to amend their ways. But he paid the price for this when a thug, hired by a nobleman who had been deprived of his pleasures, assaulted him and left him for dead in the middle of the street. Some millers picked him up and brought him to Inés's house, where he remained laid up for almost two whole months. He was in such a sorry state that whenever they made his bed they had to use towels to move him. They cured him by wrapping him in sheets soaked in wine. He never indicated who might have been the perpetrator or the instigator of this act of revenge. Juan recalled that during these days, 'My mother treated and coddled him as if he were her own son or an angel come to earth; she stayed by him during the night without ever sleeping a wink.... The flower of Barcelona's nobility came to visit him, both ladies and gentlemen, and they all pampered him to death.'

RADIANT

Ignatius's person radiated something that brought out veneration and affection in others. Many made mention of a light that lit up his face, a physical transparency of an intense interior light. The most remarkable testimony of this was given by Isabel Roser. She saw the pilgrim for the first time in Barcelona prior to his departure for Jerusalem in 1523, seated on the church steps surrounded by children. She was struck by a light that shone forth from the pilgrim's pallid and somewhat luminous face. She heard a voice from within say, 'Call him!' With her husband's permission, she sent for the pilgrim and invited him to dine with her family, who asked him to speak to them about God. He told them that he was on the point of embarking on a ship, but they took his books off the boat, which then departed, only to sink while still in sight of Barcelona. Isabel would always remain fond of the pilgrim, and years later, during the time he was in Paris, she would help him to defray the cost of his schooling. In 1532, he would write the following words of gratitude to her from Paris: 'I owe more to you than to any other person I know in this life.'

GATHERING COMPANIONS

While studying in Barcelona, Ignatius 'began to have the desire to gather certain persons to himself in order to put into operation the plan he had, beginning at that time, of helping to repair the defects he saw in people's service of God, namely, persons who might be like trumpets of Jesus Christ'. This is the first indication of his reforming ideal. Three companions joined him, but their enthusiasm would dim with time, so that he lost them to other interests. Meanwhile Ignatius's teacher, Ardevol, was pressing him to begin his studies of arts at Alcalá. He left Barcelona late in 1525, leaving behind him a profound spiritual heritage – people touched by his unique personality, and places and objects where his lingering presence hovered. A letter of his to Inés Pascual, dated 6 December 1525, warned her of some serious problems facing her, and advised her on how she might avoid them and 'live joyfully'. This man, so exacting when it came to himself, showed himself lenient when it came to his adopted mother: she should not resort to excessive penance as he had done. He signed his letter, 'The poor pilgrim, Ignatius'.

How much do you desire that others would come to know God?

25. Student at Alcalá, 1526-27

Ignatius 'left all alone for Alcalá' and arrived there around March 1526. In his *Autobiography,* he does not give his personal reasons for entering on this course of studies, which lasted almost a year and a half. He was progressing toward an uncertain future with joy, and with the same joy he welcomed each day with all the pleasures and sufferings that it brought. At a time when the call from the Americas was awakening greed for quick and easy riches, he persisted in his wish to be unknown and to live in total poverty. He had nothing of his own. He had freed himself from all dependencies. We cannot say that he possessed a rich interior life, but rather that a rich interior life possessed him. He was ever aware of the companionship of God and the presence of Christ, who dominated his being. His existence was defined not by having, but rather by being. This happiness of being came from the joy of loving, sharing and giving.

ALCALÁ

'As soon as he arrived at Alcalá, he began to beg and live on alms.' He registered on the roster of poor students. Finally, some people walking with a priest came across the pilgrim begging in his customary way, and began to poke fun at him and insult him 'as they usually do with the hale and hearty who take to begging'. At this very moment, the superintendent of the hospice happened to pass by. Filled with disgust and shame, he invited the pilgrim to stay at the hospice. 'He gave him a room and all he needed', which meant food, a bed and a candle. Thus provided, it seemed that he had all he needed to concentrate on his studies, but in fact he gave other projects greater priority. 'During his stay at Alcalá, he was busy giving spiritual exercises and teaching Christian doctrine and in so doing gave glory to God. There were many persons who came to a full knowledge and delight in spiritual things.' Whatever he said and did 'caused much talk among the people, especially because of the crowds that came wherever he taught catechism'. He was a past master of the simple word directly delivered, without any padding and rhetorical styles.

HERETICS?

In the year prior to his arrival in Alcalá, that is, in 1525, the Inquisition moved in with force against groups called 'The Enlightened' (*alumbrados*). These would meet together to read the Bible and other books; they preferred mental to vocal prayer, and distanced themselves from the customary devotions of ordinary Christians. They claimed to be moved by intense mystical communication on the part of the Holy Spirit, especially those of them called 'The perfect'. They glossed over ascetical practices and aspired to the highest degrees of spiritual freedom, which sometimes encouraged them to indulge in the grossest sins of the flesh. They repudiated the mediation of the Church, specifically the hierarchy and the sacraments, while seeking direct communication with God.

'IN THE MANNER OF THE APOSTLES'

It was no wonder that the Inquisitors suspected that the pilgrim's meetings were simply repetitions of the alumbrados' meetings that had been stifled the previous year. Two officials of the Inquisition arrived in Alcalá to investigate Ignatius and his followers. It was said that the officials 'were going to make mincemeat of them'. In November 1526, Ignatius was told by the vicar that the judges found nothing reproachable in what he and his Alcalá companions taught, nor in their lives, nor had they any objection to their continuing what they had been doing. At the same time, the vicar found fault with the fact that Ignatius and his companions were going about as a group, dressed in habits, despite the fact that they were not religious. He ordered that two of them should dye their clothes black, and the other two dye theirs yellowish-brown. This was the first time that Ignatius had collided with the Church, and he took advantage of the situation to complain about a priest who had refused to give one of the group Holy Communion, on the basis that this person received the sacrament on a weekly basis, which seemed too frequent to the priest. He who welcomed poverty, contempt and humiliation would not tolerate anyone trifling with his orthodoxy. 'We would like to know if they found any heresy in us,' Ignatius said. 'No,' replied the vicar, 'if they had, they would have burned you.' 'They would likewise have burned you,' retorted the pilgrim, 'if they found heresy in you.' The poor accused dyed their clothes. Later, the vicar ordered the pilgrim not to go barefoot, and 'he did this without any fuss, as in matters of this kind when he was given a command'. He was satisfied to live with his companions simply, 'in the manner of the apostles'. Did such a mode of life constitute the seed of the future Society of Jesus?

PREACHING IN PRISON

The companions studied the principles of grammar and logic, and met together at certain times, joined by some women. In these mysterious meetings, Ignatius was adapting his Spiritual Exercises to his devout followers.

These meetings also became the object of suspicion, and further investigations followed. A constable came on one occasion to fetch Ignatius, and he threw him into prison. He was jailed for almost a month and a half. His visitors still came and worked hard to have him released. But this strange prisoner wanted no help from anyone, and his only answer to their offers was, 'He for whose love I have come here will set me free whenever it is to his service.' Like Saint Paul in his Roman prison, Ignatius converted his into a theatre of operation, doing the same things he had done when he moved about freely: namely, teaching catechism and giving his Spiritual Exercises. His freedom knew no limits and his mastery of these adverse circumstances was the fruit of his interior self-assurance.

The superintendent of the hospice gave Ignatius a room and all he needed, food, a bed and a candle.

Teaching in jail

Recall the people who have cared for you and been generous to you.

26. The Inquisition

MARY OF THE FLOWER

In May 1527, while Ignatius was still in prison in Alcalá, the vicar, Figueroa, began interrogating witnesses in an effort to get to the bottom of the case against him. The first was Maria de la Flor, Mary of the Flower – a lovely sounding name for one who 'once had been a woman of ill repute, who went around with many of the enrolled students, and who was lost', as she described herself. Intrigued by the private conversations that went on between Ignatius and her aunt and other women, she came to realise that they were in the habit of telling the pilgrim about their troubles and that the pilgrim would console them and talk to them about serving God. One day she determined to see the pilgrim herself and ask him to speak to her about 'serving God'. Ignatius informed her that he would have to speak to her continuously for a whole month and that during this period she would have to go to confession and receive Holy Communion on a weekly basis. He warned her that she would experience days of great interior joy, 'and that she would not know from where this joy would come', and that on other days she would experience profound sadness. It was in these ups and downs that the secret of her advancement could be found, for these were the signs of deep resonance within her spirit to the touch of God. Ignatius was not alarmed by these highs and lows of the spirit, and placed such confidence in his spiritual remedy that he told her, if at the end of the month she was still not cured, she could go back to the life that she had been living! Maria's long, meticulous deposition to the Inquisitor is of extraordinary psychological value. She was all emotion, all sentiment. As she spoke of her sins, desires, interior struggles, and even about those dark zones of her conscience about which she was not fully aware, she remained totally transparent.

RESPECT

Ignatius's pedagogy must have been to go slowly with Maria, and, in the beginning, to stick to what was purely elementary. He supported her when she experienced the desolation that was the result of the first steps she was taking in the interior life. Ignatius was perhaps the first man who did not regard Maria as an object, who spoke to her about propositions different from selling her body and enjoying sexual pleasure. He taught her the

Commandments, got her to give up her habit of swearing, to make an examination of conscience twice a day, and to thank God for his goodness. Ignatius gave this young woman, who had been better schooled by life's misadventures than by moral theology, the most fundamental and practical norms of morality. He introduced her to the simple methods of prayer spelled out in the Spiritual Exercises. He had confidence in his methodology, in God's grace and in men and women. He was a guide, trustworthy, far seeing and down to earth.

MOTHER AND DAUGHTER

What alarmed Figueroa most were the bodily convulsions that were taking place among the women who followed Ignatius. Ignatius replied that these swooning fits were reflections of the interior resistance and repugnance they felt taking place within them as they changed their lives. For his part, Ignatius said that he encouraged the women to persevere and be strong, and he assured them that such temptations would disappear after a few months, since 'he had experienced the same himself'. Figueroa then broached the subject of the recent disappearance of a certain mother and daughter. Ignatius acknowledged that he knew them, but swore that he never knew of their plans to leave Alcalá until they had already gone. The vicar's suspicious attitude began to lift. 'Placing his hand on the pilgrim's shoulder, as a sign of his satisfaction, he said: "This was the reason why you have been imprisoned."' The mother and daughter were in fact widows and the latter was 'very young and attractive'. They were aristocrats intent on going by foot and alone to the shrine in Andalucía where the veil of Saint Veronica was kept. They would beg all along the way.

Ignatius spent considerable time speaking man to man with the vicar about this case. The fact was that these two women had told him that they were determined to travel about the world, going from hospice to hospice in the service of the poor. He had always dissuaded them from such an undertaking because the daughter was so young and attractive, and had told them that they could visit the sick and poor without leaving Alcalá. Three days later, the women reappeared after a six-week absence. They said that they had made their pilgrimage on their own initiative, without seeking advice from anyone. The mother admitted that she had spoken with Ignatius on a number of occasions and she considered him 'a good person and a servant of God'. The daughter had spoken with him several times. In his *Autobiography*, Ignatius described the two as women who 'made great progress in the spiritual life, especially the daughter'.

'They were closing the door to him in helping souls.'

FORBIDDEN TO TEACH

In early June 1527, Ignatius and his companions were given the judgement of the vicar. He and his fellow-accused were absolutely forbidden for a three-year period to teach anyone, either publicly or privately, individually or in groups. The reason was not because of any doctrinal irregularities in what they had taught, but because, as Ignatius had stated, 'they had no learning'. He himself acknowledged that 'the pilgrim was the most educated of the group', and then added, 'though his learning had little foundation, and this was the first thing he usually mentioned when anyone examined him'. Ignatius was unhappy about the sentence, but he accepted it. 'As a result of this sentence, he was somewhat doubtful about what he should do, since it seemed they were closing the door to him in helping souls, without giving him any reason except that he had not studied. At last he decided to go to the Archbishop of Toledo and put the case in his hands.' Ignatius was not a man who was easily defeated. He did not clearly see as yet that, for such spiritual ministries, knowledge was desirable and necessary.

How do you react when your efforts to do good are frustrated?

27. Frustrations in Salamanca, 1527

COLDER THAN ICE

While Ignatius was in Alcalá, the writings of Erasmus of Rotterdam were being read widely. Both men were concerned about the Church. But the biting public criticism, the satirical and outrageous liberties of Erasmus that made his admirers roar with laughter would have found a gut reaction of disapproval with Ignatius, who was the most successful but also the most silent of the reformers of that century. Ignatius was in agreement with Luther, who had said that the words of Erasmus were 'colder than ice'. Erasmus rejected the authority of the Church and had the habit of making himself the centre of discussion in debated issues. Ignatius, who read only what he was looking for, did not find satisfaction in Erasmus, who had never posed to himself Ignatius's dramatic challenge, 'What ought I do for Christ?'

TO SALAMANCA

Around 20 June 1527, Ignatius and his companions departed from Alcalá. For many years afterward, he would be bedevilled by the rumour that his flight was occasioned by the fact that he was going to be burned at the stake. But Ignatius did not flee; rather, he was taking the battle to the Archbishop of Toledo himself. However, the latter, while receiving Ignatius in friendly fashion, did not lift the sentence. Instead, he gave Ignatius some money and recommended him to some of his friends at Salamanca.

DINNER TALK

When he was an old man, Ignatius dedicated nine paragraphs in his *Autobiography* to Salamanca, but what he said in them was limited to events that had very little to do with the glory of its great University. Ignatius had arrived in the early part of July 1527, and his four companions had already got there a few days earlier. He chose a Dominican confessor, who told him after twelve days: 'The fathers of the house would like to speak with you.' On the following Sunday, Ignatius and Calixto, one of his companions, came to dinner. Calixto was dressed in a short gown with a large hat and boots that reached half way up his calves; moreover, he was carrying a long staff. Even Ignatius acknowledged that his friend offered a ridiculous sight for all to behold. Furthermore, since he was very tall, he looked all the more hilarious.

Some of the priests went with them to a chapel after they had eaten, where the sub-prior proceeded to make some favourable comments on what he had heard about the type of life his guests were leading – that 'they went about preaching like the apostles'. The friars expressed the wish to learn more details about their manner of life. One of them asked Calixto about the way he was dressed. Then Ignatius told them of how they had suffered in the prison at Alcalá, and how they were forbidden to dress as religious. He hid nothing about how weak his academic foundations were. He stated that they did not preach, but spoke about God, virtues and vices. 'You are not educated men and yet you speak of virtues and vices! Therefore you must be speaking through the power of the Holy Spirit. Now, precisely what comes to you from the Holy Spirit is what we would like to know more about.' After a short discussion, Ignatius replied, 'Father, I will not say more, except before my superiors who can oblige me to do so.' To this the response was: 'Very well, then stay here. We can easily make you tell us all.'

IMPRISONED

So they stayed three days in the convent, chatting with the friars, who became divided about Ignatius. A notary then appeared and took them to a common prison, where they were put in irons. Later, the other companions were also imprisoned. Ignatius handed over his Spiritual Exercises for examination. Twenty-two days of confinement passed, during which time Ignatius received physical and moral support from many friends. Finally, the judgement came: they could continue to speak of the things of God but not define mortal and venial sin. Ignatius responded that he would accept this verdict while in Salamanca but that the judges 'were closing his mouth and making it impossible for him to help his neighbour in the best way he could'.

TO HELP PEOPLE

Released from prison on 22 August 1527, Ignatius had, it seemed, to start his life again from scratch. 'He began to commend the matter to God and to *think of what he ought to do.*' Like John of the Cross a few years later, he thought of joining a decadent religious order so that he could suffer and perhaps also help in its reform. But he wanted 'to help people, and in order to accomplish this he would study, and then gather together a few companions animated by the same desire, while keeping those he already had'. He would go to Paris to study, while his companions would continue in Salamanca until they could join him. So he set out for Paris in January 1528, alone and on foot. His friend Inés Pascual tried as best she could to get him sufficient travelling provisions. He accepted a letter of credit extended by a merchant that would enable him to cash a certain amount of money in Paris to cover his initial expenses, while other friends in Salamanca promised to send him help while he was in studies.

Ignatius wanted to help people, so he would study and then gather together a few companions.

How available are you to what God might want you to do?

28. Student in Paris, 1528-34

ALONE AND ON FOOT

Having walked from Salamanca to Barcelona, Ignatius set out at the beginning of 1528 for Paris 'alone and on foot', and arrived there on 2 February 1528. It was the height of winter and the journey was long. One month later, he wrote to Inés Pascual in Barcelona to tell her that the journey had gone well and to thank her for the good will and affection she had shown him. He asked to be remembered to her son, and did not forget to extend a grateful greeting to her neighbour, who must have slipped a few little gifts in his travelling bag at the moment of his departure. He added: 'I shall study until the Lord asks me to do something else.' Ignatius was a serious student at this stage. He was now thirty-seven and he had come to the conclusion that he had advanced too quickly in his former studies and 'found his knowledge of the fundamentals very shaky'. And so he signed up to take courses in Latin at a Paris College. This was a mandatory preparatory course, where one obtained skills in grammar, rhetoric and versification. The pupils in this class were very young, some only ten years old. He does not exaggerate a bit in the *Autobiography* when he says that he 'attended classes with young boys and made progress according to the prescribed curriculum of Paris'.

A POOR AND VAGRANT STUDENT

Even though he was not a typical, run-of-the-mill student, Ignatius was able, for the first time in his life, to devote himself to his studies without worrying about money. What he had brought with him from Barcelona was enough for two years in Paris. But for safekeeping he turned over all the money he had to a Spaniard who was living in the same boarding house, and this man recklessly spent it all, leaving Ignatius penniless barely two months after arriving in Paris. So he had to leave his boarding house to beg in the Paris streets – not the first student in history nor the last to pursue this time-honoured practice. Ignatius was accepted at the pilgrim hospice of Saint-Jacques, but this presented him with another problem, namely how to continue his studies at his College, which was two miles away. The times for opening and closing the doors at either institution were rigorous but not synchronised: class began at 4 a.m., but Ignatius could not get out of the hospice before sunrise. He had to cut down on class time and also give some study time for begging. The inevitable result was that he saw that 'he was making little progress in his studies'. He tried to find a part-time job as a domestic servant to some professor, but despite his best efforts no one was able to find an employer for him. Through experience, Ignatius came to taste the despair that is so much part of the life of the ordinary poor student.

BEGGING TRIPS

In the end, Ignatius took some realistic advice from a Spanish friar, who told him about the generosity of the Spanish merchants in Flanders and advised him to contact them. Ignatius decided that it was worth missing classes to go up to Flanders and stay there for two months every year, provided that these excursions did indeed help him to defray the cost of his studies. During Lent of 1529, and during the summers of 1530 and 1531, he undertook trips to Bruges and Antwerp. In 1531, he travelled as far as London, which turned out to be his most remunerative trip. His repeated trips to Flanders eventually gained him the good will of protectors, who, by sending him letters of credit in Paris, saved him the pain of having to walk all the way to Flanders to beg for alms. His unfortunate experience with the Spaniard who had cheated him made him more cautious, although no less charitable on that account. He instructed the man in Paris who exchanged his bills of credit to cover the needs of other impoverished students as well as his own.

MISJUDGEMENT?

In Bruges, Ignatius was invited to dine with Luis Vives, the famous humanist from Valencia and an admirer of Erasmus. It was Lent, and therefore a day of abstinence, so the main dish was an exquisitely prepared fish dish. Vives began the dinner conversation by making comments on the scant penitential significance of observing the Church's law on abstaining from meat. Ignatius, who as a rule spoke little while eating, took a stand contrary to his host on this occasion and spoke his mind with an unexpected line of reasoning: 'You and others who have the means to do so can dine on deliciously prepared fish without, perhaps, profiting from the Church's purpose for abstinence. But such is not the case with the majority of people for whom the Church cares. These people cannot be as exquisite as you; they find abstinence a means to mortify their bodies and to do penance.' Ignatius here comes across as a poor, obscure man acquainted with difficult penances, who lived much closer to the ordinary people than did Vives. Vives came away with a very high opinion of Ignatius, and confessed to a close friend that he had discovered a saint, even a founder of a future religious order. However, Ignatius seems to have come away with a poor impression of Vives. At a later date, he would forbid members of the Society to read Vives's works, as well as the writings of

Ignatius tasted the despair that is so much part of the life of the ordinary poor and vagrant student.

Erasmus. Ignatius did not know that this man, with his suspect opinions on bodily mortification, had forfeited a handsome sinecure at the richly endowed Corpus Christi College, Oxford, for opposing the divorce of Henry VIII. Despite having lost his parents and grandparents in the Jewish persecution orchestrated by the Spanish Inquisition, Vives was a man of exacting principles, who would one day write a beautiful treatise, *A Defence of the Christian Faith*, which is a profession of faith in and fidelity to the Catholic Church.

How do you react when cheated or betrayed?

Student in Paris

29. A Man of Influence, Paris 1529

GIVING THE EXERCISES

In May and June of 1529, Ignatius was in a position to give up his habit of begging for a while, so he 'began to give himself more intensively than usual to spiritual conversations' as a way of compensating for his newly found free time; but these conversations were not with the small boys from his humanities classes nor were they limited to in-between class time. On the contrary, he gave his Spiritual Exercises to three outstanding students, all of them Spaniards. His influence on each was spectacular. Their lives were so radically changed that their behaviour became a topic of conversation throughout Paris. After completing the Exercises, these three university men began giving everything they had to the poor, including their books. They then moved into a hospice and took to begging in streets all over the city. Since two of them were academic celebrities in their own right, their change of heart caused 'a great disturbance' throughout the University, particularly among the Spanish students.

BLAMED

The students' friends and relatives tried to dissuade them from their bizarre ways of acting, and, when verbal persuasion had no effect, they dragged them physically away from the hospice. After this incident, the two men agreed to finish their studies, and then they could go back to the way they had been living. But the conversion of one of them provoked the hostility of his rector at Sainte-Barbe, who declared before all that Ignatius had turned one of his students into a madman. He accused Ignatius of being a 'seducer of students', and even threatened to have him publicly flogged the first time he showed his face at Sainte-Barbe. Thus Ignatius was held responsible for the unexpected life-choices of his companions and he became the object of much gossip and suspicion. 'I was held responsible for everything,' he wrote in a letter of 1542. What was the secret of his influence? Everything lay in what he said and in what he did; in how he said it and how he did it; in how he gave himself to others. Ignatius took seriously and loved sincerely those who listened to what he had to say, those who became his followers, but also those who were his persecutors, and even those who took advantage of what he said and how he loved.

RECKLESS LOVE

Take, for example, the case of the Spaniard who had gone off and spent all the money Ignatius had entrusted to him when he first came to Paris – money that would have kept Ignatius living comfortably for two whole years.

This fellow disappeared one day from Paris and the next thing that was heard of him was that he was on his way back to Spain. However, when he got to Rouen, where he had intended to book his passage home, he fell ill. He wrote a letter to Ignatius informing him of his situation and his need, and Ignatius, who in his youth had never hated anyone, on this occasion showed himself not only generous and forgiving, but even conceived the notion of going off to visit and help this reckless youth. He made his decision with a higher and more noble purpose. 'He thought he might induce the Spaniard to leave the world and give himself entirely to the service of God.' It was then that a madly generous idea crossed his mind: he would walk barefoot all the way from Paris to Rouen, eating or drinking nothing until he got there. But was this tempting God? He considered the question in the quiet of the chapel in the convent of Saint-Dominique, and then in peace he made up his mind.

CONSOLED

The next morning he got up very early to put his resolution into practice, but, as he was getting dressed, his feeling revolted so much against the idea that he was all but paralysed. Still fighting this repugnance, he left the hospice at dawn and began his journey. He came to a small church in Argenteuil, where, according to tradition, the seamless robe of Christ was kept. At this point of the journey, Ignatius was still prey to the dread and aversion that had been his ever since he began his journey, but the recollection of this seamless robe with its concrete reference to Jerusalem and to Christ's passion and death had a purifying effect on his spirit. Like a bad dream, his anguish disappeared and 'so great a joy and spiritual consolation came upon him that he began to cry out and talk with God'.

LAVISH FORGIVENESS

On the first evening, Ignatius bedded down with a poor beggar in a hospice. The next night, he took shelter in a hay barn; and on the third day, 'after eating and drinking nothing and barefoot just as he had planned', he arrived in Rouen. Unquestionably, this man with will-power of steel was a most austere person; he was the incarnation of those knights, so common in the Middle Ages, who went out to assist the needy. In three days, he had been able to cover 150 kilometres – close to 100 miles – without eating or drinking anything. This in itself is an astonishing record worthy of an athlete. But in signalling out the physical achievement, we should not underestimate the moral exploit accomplished. Ignatius brought consolation to the sick man who had such a heavy heart; he booked him on a ship bound for Spain and gave him letters of introduction to his friends. He offered no reasons wrapped in devious arguments. He simply acted; that was all.

Ignatius would walk barefoot all the way from Paris to Rouen, eating or drinking nothing.

Can you recall instances when you were treated with reckless generosity? Have you ever done the same for others?

30. Study and Action in Paris, 1528-34

IGNATIUS THE DANCER

Ignatius could act in ways that were less physically demanding and spectacular than walking from Paris to Rouen, and the following incident reveals yet another side of his complex character. Out of prudishness, this story was deleted from his first official biography in 1572 and was forgotten until 1965.

A certain Jesuit was very sick and depressed as a result of a malady. Ignatius paid him a visit and asked him if there was anything that he could do to dispel his gloom and sadness. The sick man said that there was just one thing that he could think of that would help him feel better: 'If you could sing a little and dance a little as they do in your country, I think this could give me some consolation.'

Ignatius replied: 'Would that make you happy?'

'Oh, yes, very happy,' said the sick man.

Ignatius, despite his limp, did what the sick man asked. When he had finished, he said: 'Please do not ask me to do that again, because I shall not do it.' The sick man was so overjoyed by Ignatius's charity that, after he left, the depression that was eating up his heart was lifted; he began to improve, and was soon cured.

ABANDONED

The four companions whom Ignatius had left behind in Salamanca did not remain in his company but went their separate ways. Ignatius had kept in touch with them by letter from Paris, but he told them of 'the slight chance there was of his bringing them to Paris to study'. One found his fortune in Mexico, while another returned to his home town of Segovia, where 'he began to live in such a way that he seemed to have forgotten his earlier resolves'. The third was appointed to a bishopric in Mexico, but died a tragic death on his arrival, while the last became a Franciscan. Time clarifies and fathoms the mysteries of the human heart and the consistency of its desires. Ignatius's seductive power was no guarantee that initial fidelity would withstand every assault. When deprived of his presence, the group that constituted the Alcalá and Salamanca companions faded away, as did the Paris trio whom he had converted to a godly life. Ignatius, for all that, did not give up his attempt to look for companions.

CLEARED BY THE INQUISITION

On his return from Rouen in September 1529, Ignatius discovered that a complaint had been made about him to the Inquisition in regard to the weird happenings surrounding this Paris trio. Instead of waiting until he was summoned, Ignatius showed up before the Inquisitor and told him that he knew that he was looking for him. He said that he was eager to cooperate with the Inquisitor, and, to the astonishment of the latter, he presented him with all the information and details he sought. Ignatius then asked him to deal quickly with his case because he wanted to begin the new university term in peace and free from any involvement with the Inquisition. The Inquisitor, a Dominican, admitted that he had indeed received a complaint, but he showed no concern about the case and allowed the intrepid student to go free.

Ignatius began his course in Arts or Humanities on 1 October 1529 in the College of Sainte-Barbe. This College had earlier threatened him with a public flogging should he show up, for having transgressed its rules under the pretext of religion. The student body had already been convoked to witness this deplorable spectacle, at which point Ignatius went to speak with the fearsome rector. He himself did not mind the personal humiliation, but, as a guide and apostle, he worried that his followers would not be able to bear such a trial. It took apparently only a few minutes for his persuasive words to change the rector's mind and turn him into a friend. Many years later, it would be the same rector who would open to the Society the doors to India. How ironic are the ways of providence!

SERIOUS STUDY

To the great surprise of observers, Ignatius moderated his apostolic work and gave himself over to serious study. One day, one of his teachers ventured to tell him 'that he was surprised that he was getting along quietly without anyone causing him trouble'. Ignatius fired back a blunt comment, saying, 'The reason is because I do not speak of the things of God, but once this course is over, I'll go back to my old ways.' He studied, not with enthusiasm but with stubborn adult tenacity. Philosophy and theology did stir up in him the esteem and respect that they can provoke in anyone who approaches them in a methodical way. No form of unadulterated spiritualism could substitute for them. From his painful apprenticeship as a student, Ignatius would later be able to draw some practical consequences, which would later have profound consequences for many others. He taught Jesuit students that a man should appreciate academic learning; be convinced of the need to integrate Scripture, the teaching of the Church Fathers and the wisdom of scholasticism; have a feel for pedagogical methods and appreciate the value of academic degrees in the world in which he lives; and that students must be given the minimal conditions to enable them to dedicate themselves totally to study.

Study then he did, but an intellectual he was not, nor did he want to be one. Ignatius was a man who radiated activity. Never would he astonish his masters by the subtleties of his thought, but he would overwhelm them by the mastery he showed when speaking about theological matters. *There was something about the spell of his personality that gave him a certain command over his fellow-students and even over his professors.* He was not a glib or brilliant conversationalist who was able to win the superficial sympathies of others. Instead, wherever he went he created a ferment, sowing restlessness; he drew the attention of others and, what was more important, he transformed his environment and those in it.

There was something about the spell of his personality that gave Ignatius a certain command over his fellow-students and even over his professors.

Are you aware of any gifts in yourself for helping others to find God?

31. The Art of Spiritual Conversation

HELPING OTHERS TO CONVERSION

Exteriorly, there was nothing special in the way Ignatius came across to others. He knew nothing about the skills of oratory. In initiating a conversation, he was specific and to the point, and his speech was devoid of all those precious affectations so characteristic of the academic world of that time. He himself had been converted; he knew that in dealing with another, the breakdown point had to be reached before there could be a surrender, a self-giving, and so he was not afraid to get down to essentials. The past had to be liquidated or, to put it more simply and provocatively, the person had to make a general confession. The break with the ambiguous or sinful present had to take place; evil companions and bad habits had to be given up; the person had to become free from unhelpful influences and take a firm stand as required against anything and anyone. The symbol of this break with the past, this liberation, was weekly Confession and Communion and attending the meetings led by Ignatius. The symbol was simple and yet it implied a commitment. Once this occurred, other more profound changes could take place, and Ignatius stuck to the techniques of his Exercises to bring about these changes.

THE SECRET

The secret of Ignatius's attraction resided in the authenticity of what he said and how he lived, in the example he gave, and in the direct way he dealt with others. There was nothing deceitful or artificial about him. He was a committed man. People could always go to him when they needed material help, advice, encouragement or support. His secretary, Polanco, recreated the atmosphere surrounding Ignatius at this time of his life when he wrote that Ignatius 'lived in peace with everyone, even with those who had the spirit of the world'. He spoke with persons of influence in order to help students. He came to the aid of his impoverished fellow-students by giving them alms or by helping to get them jobs with teachers who could give them a room for study. He helped them by getting them subsidies, or just by giving them good advice. His circle of friends, made up both of benefactors and of those who received financial help from him, was large indeed. At his advice, more than one of these entered the religious life. The Principal of a neighbouring College was so impressed by Ignatius's teaching that he wanted to confer the degree of doctor of theology on this lay student who, he stated, was teaching theology to him.

Ignatius's presence, which for the most part was low key and discreet, could, at times, expand to the point where it manifested itself in courageous action. On one occasion, wanting a man to leave the woman with whom he was living, he waited for him on the outskirts of Paris. As the man passed by, Ignatius threw himself into an icy pond in an effort to rid the man of his passion. We do not know if this penitential act had the desired effect. Again, to win over a bad priest, Ignatius went to confession to him and told him about his own sins, stressing what steps he took to repent of them.

COURAGE

Again, Ignatius went to inspect a plague-stricken house on behalf of a student. To console one of the lodgers there who was sick, he placed his hand on the man's sores, 'and this action made the man feel a bit better'. Afterward, when he was by himself, Ignatius noticed that his hand began to hurt, and he became obsessed by the fear that he had contracted the plague. His imagination became so strong that he could hardly control it, and, finally, in order to put an end to his apprehensions, he thrust the sore hand into his mouth. The result was that he was quarantined from the College for several days. Modern psychology recognises in his action a paradoxical intention, which, even if it does not always infallibly cure obsessive-compulsive behaviour patterns, is at least an efficacious remedy against those in which anxiety is an underlying factor.

MARTIN LUTHER

Such were some of the activities Ignatius resorted to during his Paris days. They are described in the pages of his *Autobiography*, which is singularly meagre when it comes to giving details about what was taking place at the University and in the world at large. It is true that he was immersed in his inner world, in his immediate academic concerns and in his eagerness to guide others to discover their own interior world. But it was impossible for him to be impervious to events in the world about him. The Paris of his day was growing inflexible against Lutheranism. In 1521, the year of Ignatius's conversion, Luther was condemned; two years later, his books were burned on the square in front of Notre Dame and the sale of his writings was proscribed. Certain Lutherans were burned at the stake and others died after having had their tongues cut out or pierced. The writings of Erasmus were condemned. The word 'Protestant' was used for the first time in 1529. A fanatic Lutheran decapitated a statue of the Virgin Mary, an incident that caused such public consternation that the King himself was moved to make solemn public reparation during a magnificent procession through the streets of Paris. At the time, none of these things seemed to have had any effect on Ignatius, but they did indeed make his attachment to the Church more binding, secure, profound and unqualified. Despite the diatribes that Luther and Erasmus were venting on religious life, Ignatius continued to direct people to the cloister.

HOW TO SERVE GOD?

Why did he himself not follow the same path? According to Polanco, 'he won the love of many, keeping in mind his desire of attracting some suitable individuals for his own project'. Ignatius himself wrote that when he began his Arts courses in 1529, he determined to restrict his conversations to those who were intent on serving God, 'but he would not try to add to their number, as he wanted to give himself to his studies'. What he meant by 'serving God' was probably unclear to himself at this time, but would unfold later.

The secret of Ignatius's attraction resided in the authenticity of what he said and how he lived.

Spiritual conversation

Do you find yourself authentic in what you say and how you live?

32. New Companions, 1529

UNEXPECTED ENCOUNTERS

Ignatius's life was full of unexpected encounters, which had long-lasting consequences. He seems to have been a man sure of the final results, who cast his net in all directions without knowing the exact moment of the happy catch and, at the same time, without being daunted by failures. Among his many encounters, two stand out because of their singular consequences. After being admitted to Sainte-Barbe, he shared a room with two students who were soon to receive their degrees, Pierre Favre and Francis Xavier. The first fertile seed of what was to be the Society of Jesus began with the conversations that took place in this room. The *Autobiography* entry on the beginning of this group is limited to these laconic words: 'During this period he was carrying on conversations with Master Pierre Favre and Master Francis Xavier, both of whom he later won to God's service through the Exercises.'

PIERRE FAVRE

Pierre Favre was a blond young man with a soul as pure as the alpine heights of his native Savoy. Born in 1506, the son of peasants, he had been a shepherd during his childhood days. His desire to study was supported by one of his uncles, who was a Carthusian. He came to Paris in 1525, four years before Ignatius. Favre was gifted with a special goodness and a natural sympathy for all, and he had a real charm about him. He helped Ignatius, his new and elder roommate, with his studies. When he wrote his *Memorial* (1542–46), he praised God for having allowed him to meet Ignatius. They passed from small talk to deep spiritual conversations, till the tutor and the old student had to cut these short so that they could be faithful to their studies. A deep friendship was born, sustained by a common life, for they were roommates who shared their meals and money.

One day, Favre, who was shy, uncertain and tortured by scruples, allowed Ignatius to penetrate into the intimate recesses of his being. Although Ignatius was an apprentice when it came to logic, he knew a great deal about what Favre was telling him, and he helped his friend to attain peace, a gift that has no price. He spoke to him about the knowledge of God and of oneself and how to understand one's conscience. From that moment on, Favre kept no secrets from him. Ignatius had put to rest in the angelic young man sensual temptations that had been tormenting him. Favre knew the meaning of fornication only through his reading; others in his world knew it through experience, like one of the professors on the College faculty who had died several years earlier from syphilis.

Besides his scruples, Favre was undecided about his future. But soon he identified completely with the ideals of his friend and counsellor. He wrote: 'We came *to be one* in wish and will and firm purpose of embracing the kind of life we are now living.' Ignatius spent four years working on the spiritual crafting of Favre, who ended up by choosing to follow the same form of life as his friend, and became a valiant and tireless worker and one of the pillars of the young Society.

FRANCIS XAVIER

Francis Xavier was the same age as Pierre Favre, twenty-three, when he met Ignatius. He had been at Sainte-Barbe since 1 October 1525. Favre and himself had been roommates for four years. Xavier was friendly, jovial, outgoing and energetic and a fine athlete. By nature a dreamer, he wanted to compensate through his own personal triumphs for the rough times his family had undergone, for he had grown up in a family that had been ruined. When he was twelve years old, he watched the towers of the family castle being torn down at the orders of the King of Spain. Ignatius had been an enemy of the Xavier family at Pamplona in 1521, but all of that was already a thing of the past. Now the road to be taken by the youngest son of the Xavier family seemed to be clearly marked. Soon after Ignatius arrived at Sainte-Barbe, Xavier received his licentiate. Shortly afterward, he became a Master and a member of the Faculty of Arts. He took steps to prove his nobility and secured appointment as a canon in Pamplona. A Navarrese student became his serving man. He must have been a bit short on money to meet all the demands of his new position because the academic award cost him dearly and his family was in no position to assist him regularly or generously.

Ignatius helped Xavier with money; moreover, he went out of his way to find him pupils, whom he personally introduced to him. Ignatius understood him: he had known personally the attractiveness of ambition; of being more, of having more, of being worth more; he knew what it meant to want honours, prestige and glory. Just as steady drops of water eventually wear away the hardest stone, little by little he weakened the resistance of that rock-like soul. Xavier was not in the least attracted by Ignatius's style of life, and indeed he scoffed at and made jokes about Ignatius's followers. Out of some subconscious self-defence, he kept himself at a distance from Ignatius. But slowly Ignatius dissipated his ambitions, until finally, like so much fog, they

Ignatius's life was full of unexpected encounters, which had long-lasting consequences.

evaporated altogether, enabling Xavier to attach himself to Ignatius and to make Ignatius's projects his own.

Xavier changed his life and dismissed his servant. The latter, however, decided to kill the man who had thrown a spell on his master. He went so far as to climb the stairs of the College, blinded by rage and grasping a dagger in his hand. But a single word from Ignatius was enough to cause him to fall down on his knees at Ignatius's feet. Xavier had not yet made the Exercises, but, during the first half of 1533, he had already decided to follow the way of Ignatius. He was as tough as the trees that grow in the Pyrenees, but Ignatius carved this oak-like man in a way that gave him an undying shape and grandeur. At the age of twenty-seven, these two roommates, Favre and Xavier, had already completed their apprenticeship in the spiritual life under Ignatius.

What unexpected encounters have had long-lasting consequences for you?

33. Seven Friends in Paris, 1533

LAÍNEZ

The winning over of more companions to Ignatius was more easily achieved than with Pierre Favre and Francis Xavier. Diego Laínez and Alfonso Salmerón were both very promising young men; the first was twenty-one and the second eighteen. They were close friends and eager to learn. They came from Alcalá in Spain, where they had heard about Ignatius, and they were anxious to meet him. Fate had it that the very first person Laínez met on his arrival at the place where he intended to stay in Paris was Ignatius. Ignatius's first pieces of advice about living in Paris were extremely useful to him. In no time, he became familiar with the way to get to Ignatius's residence, and he joined the group that met each Sunday. In October 1532, he had received his Master's degree from Alcalá. He was intuitive and intelligent; skilful in disputations and erudite. Physically, he was small and weak, and he had large expressive eyes. His racial origins were Jewish. He was a pious, pure and docile young man.

SALMERÓN AND BOBADILLA

Laínez's inseparable friend Salmerón was a native of Toledo. He was a frank, jolly and expansive young man, blessed with a prodigious memory, who was in the habit of reciting by heart the works of the Greek and Latin poets, which he had studied at Alcalá. Ignatius dealt separately with Laínez and Salmerón, and so, without either one knowing the intentions of the other, they eventually learned that both were committed to the same cause. Just at about the same time, Nicolás Alonso, who later would be known as Bobadilla, made his appearance in Paris. He hailed from old Castile, from the small town of Bobadilla to be exact, and he was a hothead who had a passionate, direct way of expressing himself. He held a Bachelor's degree from Alcalá and a Regent's degree from Valladolid, and he had come to Paris both because he was attracted by the reputation of the professors and because of his desire to master the languages that would enhance his theological formation. He came to Ignatius having heard that he helped students, and, as a matter of fact, Ignatius did manage to get him a job, but at the same time he warned him about the orthodoxy of the professors he had come to Paris to listen to. Bobadilla decided then to go to the Dominicans and Franciscans to study theology, and he also joined Ignatius's group.

RODRIGUES

The Portuguese Simon Rodrigues enjoyed one of the scholarships given by King John III of Portugal, and he had been living at Sainte-Barbe since 1526. In the beginning of 1529, he moved in with Ignatius, but he had no direct dealings with him in spiritual matters until 1533. As an old man in 1577, he wrote a delightful account of his Paris days. He recalled that he himself had taken the initiative to contact Ignatius because he was attracted by the sanctity of this elderly student. 'He decided to share with Ignatius some of his desires and to give him a part of his soul', and shortly afterward he became determined to follow a new way of life. This change caused consternation among his fellow Portuguese, and surprised Favre and Xavier as well.

A SINGLE DREAM

The group now numbered seven. Without knowing what the others were thinking, each of them was coming to the same resolution, namely, to go to the Holy Land and spend their life there working for the salvation of their fellow human beings, or, as Laínez would later say, and what amounts to the same thing: 'To follow the *Institute* of Ignatius.' Institute means nothing other than the way of life or the teachings of Ignatius, neither of which was yet clearly defined and certainly was not within the confines of ordinary ecclesiastical structures. This remarkable group became a homogeneous entity because its members were of the same age, shared a similar cultural background, and, most especially, had the same ideals. An intimate bonding took place, thanks to the points they shared in common and their mutual friendship. All of this began in Ignatius's room. Later, the room of each one became the room of all. On certain afternoons, they would bring food and meet together in one of the rooms to talk and dream. Ignatius was not a strategist nor was he an imposing leader; rather, he was the companion-guide who exerted a calm, strong and trustworthy type of authority and influence. He had made it possible for each one to hear God's call personally. It was curious that the call they all heard was identical to that which he himself had heard many years earlier, even down to the unpredictable detail of wanting to start their new way of life by visiting the land of Jesus.

We are now at the threshold of the adventure initiated by seven poor Christians, none of whom was a priest. Each one was master of his own fate; each had made up his own mind freely, and was now renouncing everything because he had come to one sole decision, and that was to dedicate himself to serving others. This was a generous ideal, but up to now it had no precise shape. For the time being, however, the important thing was for each of them to maintain an attitude that was completely open to whatever came along.

THE WIDER WORLD

A number of events transpired during the course of 1533 which, even though Ignatius did not make the slightest allusion to them in his *Autobiography*, should be noticed because of their historical importance. The least significant was that, on 13 March 1533, Ignatius received his licentiate in Arts, a licence to teach in Paris and throughout the world. This event must have given him some satisfaction, especially when he recalled the restrictions placed on him at Alcalá and Salamanca forbidding him to converse with others about the things of God because he did not have the academic credentials to do so. And now he was able to teach! The European event of the year was the wedding of Henry VIII and Anne Boleyn, which resulted in breaking the thousand-year-old link between England and Rome. In Paris, the plague broke out again, while Protestantism made inroads in the University, with the faculties battling against one another regarding the new doctrine.

Ignatius had made it possible for each one to hear God's call personally.

Who has helped you to hear God's personal call to you?

34. Planning a Future Together, 1534

A TOTAL OFFERING

In 1533, edicts were passed by the Parliament of Paris decreeing that anyone accused of Lutheranism by two witnesses would be tried, condemned and burned at the stake. The year 1534 began under no better auspices: the French Parliament forbade any new translations of Scripture into French. A new decree was passed, to root out heresy and to hunt down heretics.

It was in this atmosphere that Ignatius gave Pierre Favre, the first member of the group, the Spiritual Exercises, and he did this in order further to strengthen the bond between him and Favre. A few months later, Favre received Holy Orders and celebrated his first Mass on 22 July 1534. Later, all the others separately made the Exercises. These were not Exercises that led to conversion, but rather to an election or confirmation of a state in life, because even before they began them, each of his companions had already made up his mind about what he was going to be. 'It will be very profitable for those who are to go through the Exercises to enter upon them with magnanimity and generosity toward their Creator and Lord, and to offer Him their entire will and liberty, that His Divine Majesty may dispose of them and all they possess according to His most holy will.' This is the fifth annotation of Ignatius's thin book, and it is a recommendation that many people have followed religiously throughout the ages. But when was it ever carried out with greater conscientiousness than by this group, which served as the experimental group for Ignatius in judging the efficiency of his technique, the purpose of which was to make the unlimited potential of every person expand in response to the invitation of God's grace? The six companions made their retreats, one after the other. In order to do so, five of them left where they had been living and moved into a small house, where together they indulged in harsh penances and long fasts. Ignatius visited them frequently and followed up on their progress. Bobadilla was the only one who made the retreat while remaining in his room at his College.

FAMILY AFFAIRS

On 14 March 1535, Ignatius obtained the title of Master of Arts for reasons of social convenience rather than ambition or vanity. He was inscribed in the faculty of theology as Master Ignatius of Loyola, of the Diocese of Pamplona.

In June 1532, after years of silence, and perhaps in response to a letter from his brother, Ignatius had attempted to explain his adventure: 'You say you are delighted because it seems that I have taken to writing to you again after so long a period of silence. Don't be surprised. A man with a serious wound begins by applying one ointment, and then in the course of its healing another, and at the end still another. So, in the beginning of my own way one kind of ointment was necessary; then another, and, finally another type.' He wrote this letter as a warning to his family, who were obsessed with the affairs of this world and preoccupied by social success, in order to give them a taste for spiritual matters and to communicate to them the importance of doing deeds that will last for eternity. For Ignatius, blood no longer counted. He was open to all men and women. It made no difference that they were sinners, provided that they admitted this. He was interested in their immortal destiny and in the fact that they themselves should be aware of their destiny.

WHAT TO DO?
In the summer of 1534, the select group of intimate friends that had gathered around Ignatius deliberated seriously about their future. They were in no hurry to make any decision because a number of them were about to begin their theology. Whatever the future held, they concentrated now on a few specific points. They would choose actual poverty, and this presupposed that they would give up everything in order to live such a lifestyle. They would perform their ministries of helping others without charge. Once their studies were completed, their style of poverty would become more radical.

They chose to live celibate, chaste lives. In no way were they gloomy ascetics; rather, they were joyful and trusting followers of Christ, the Christ whom they had discovered and come to know through the Exercises and whose footsteps they wanted to follow in the Holy Land. One by one, they had committed themselves to make this pilgrimage, and this commitment was the most obvious, tangible link that joined them to one another. There were, of course, differences of opinion as to how it should be undertaken, but they drew up a plan of action. They would continue their courses in theology, and then, in 1537, they would leave Paris for Venice, where they would wait for a whole year, if need be, for the opportunity to board a ship for the Holy Land, but if the door to Jerusalem proved to be closed to them, they would place themselves at the disposal of the pope. If they succeeded in reaching Jesus's country, they would decide then to remain there for good or to return as a group. If they opted to return, they would take on whatever work the pope wanted them to do.

This reference to a future undertaking was what properly constituted them as a group, and, for the first time, the destiny of each was left in the hands of

The purpose of the Exercises was to make the unlimited potential of every person expand in response to the invitation of God's grace.

the group. Jerusalem was the objective: as an alternative there was Rome, but Rome was only a substitute dream for Ignatius. He had no intention whatsoever of conquering the capital of Christendom. As he had done in the affair of the Moor, Ignatius let the reins go slack because he knew that Someone else was directing his steps.

Are you aware of your potential and how God can use it?

35. Vows and Loyalty, 1534

VOWS AT MONTMARTRE

'While we were in Paris, our intention was not as yet to form a congregation, but rather to consecrate ourselves to the service of God and to help our neighbour, by living in poverty, by preaching, and by serving in hospitals.' So said Laínez many years later. As a way of confirming the decisions they had made, Ignatius and his six companions gathered at Montmartre in the Church of St Denis outside Paris on 15 August 1534, the Feast of Our Lady's Assumption. Present were Bobadilla, Favre, Ignatius, Laínez, Rodrigues, Salmerón and Xavier. Favre, the only ordained priest, celebrated the Mass. Before the Communion, each pronounced his vow one after the other, and then Favre pronounced his. Their collegial commitment thereby took on a sacred aspect. Forty years later, one of the surviving members of the group still remembered with emotion that 'holocaust' or total self-donation to God. In the vow, they included the following elements: the welfare of their neighbour; living in poverty; the pilgrimage to Jerusalem, and making themselves available to the pope if the pilgrimage was not possible, so that he might send them where he thought best.

In 1535 and 1536, on this same feast of the Assumption, they gathered at Montmartre to renew their vow. Ignatius was absent for both meetings, but in his absence three more companions joined the group: Claude Jay, who was a Savoyard, and two Frenchmen, Paschase Broët and Jean Codure. By then they numbered ten, but they were still unclear about their future. In 1537, Ignatius, who at the time was in Venice trying to find some way to embark for Jerusalem, wrote to a friend in Barcelona, saying: 'I do not know what future God our Lord holds in store for me.' In 1563, Nadal would write about this period in Ignatius's life as follows: 'He was being guided slowly toward he knew not where, and he was not thinking of founding any religious order.'

'ANOTHER MAN'

In September 1534, Xavier was finally free to make the Exercises: he retired to a small, isolated house, where Ignatius saw him quite often, and sometimes one or another of the other companions would visit with him. As penance for his athletic vanity, he bound his arms and legs so tightly with cord that it was impossible for him to move a limb; he stopped only when gangrene and amputation were looming. In spite of these excesses, the Exercises proved to be a profound and unforgettable experience for him. He came out of them with his proverbial joviality, but he was *another man*. He was never apart from his small book of the Spiritual Exercises, for it was the mould in which he had been formed. His passionate affection for Ignatius would know no bounds. He referred to him as his 'only father in the profound love of Christ', because it was thanks to Ignatius that God had spoken to him heart to heart.

RELIGIOUS WAR

In October 1534, all these 'friends in the Lord' went back to their studies. In a Dominican centre, Ignatius studied St Thomas, for whom he always had the deepest respect. That same month, Protestant placards attacking the Mass made their appearance on the walls of the capital and in other French cities. In November, the first sentences of death were handed down: condemned Lutherans, after having their tongues pierced or their hands cut off, were burned at the stake in city squares. In early 1535, it was decreed that whoever attempted to hide a Lutheran would suffer the same fate as the Lutheran, and whoever turned a Lutheran over to the authorities would receive a reward. This had become a war between irreconcilable enemies, and all doctrinal positions had to be clear and precise.

It was enough to live in Paris in that storm of opinions for Ignatius to realise that before putting people face to face with Christ in the Exercises, he first had to offer some kind of compass to enable them to hold onto their bearings. Hitherto, as we have said, the Church had been like the atmosphere that was part of his everyday living, or like a mother's lap; living *in* the Church was something natural and uncomplicated, like breathing or being healthy. He lived in the Church, not doubting her. He had no problems with authority or traditional devotions. But now he had to profess his belief in 'holy mother Church' as she really was, as history presented her, a stained Church, the Church 'militant'.

LOYALTY TO CHURCH

Ignatius believed that the Church, in spite of the weight of the centuries, continued to be 'the true spouse of Christ our Lord'. This was the living principle that animates his *Rules for Thinking with the Church* in the Exercises. He believed that one could always find reasons to criticise the Church, but also numerous reasons to defend her. Not that belief must be reduced to blind discipline. The *Rules for Thinking with the Church*, like all the rules contained in the Exercises, were meant to create a style of action for those who would adapt his Exercises in giving them to others. Originally, then, these famous rules were intended to guarantee the orthodoxy of the author of the Spiritual

Exercises. They have a general, universal soundness in coming to grips with an enduring problem, the 'true attitude of mind we ought to have in the Church militant'.

The very opposite to these rules is found in Luther and Erasmus. Confession, the Mass, the Divine Office, religious life, vows, celibacy, marriage, devotion to the saints and to relics, pilgrimages, indulgences, fasting and external penances, Lenten customs, vestments, and the whole notion of keeping secrets – all of these had been rejected by Luther and criticised by Erasmus. Ignatius, who took all of these things very seriously and made them part of his religious practice, said simply that we must praise them and not denigrate them, much less reject them. As for the hierarchical representatives of the Church, he was not about to defend the indefensible, but he sought ways to correct them without discrediting them.

Ignatius's partiality for the teaching authority of the Church was not based on rigidity or fear. Later on, he would show that he knew how to open up new frontiers, and many would be unable to accept his innovations. His *Constitutions* would be flexible and open to particular living situations and to time-tested experience. His unequivocal preference for the teaching of the Church was quite simply the result of his faith in Christ and his desire to perpetuate Christ's 'true spouse', in the manifest and ever-active presence of the Holy Spirit.

> *Ignatius believed that one could always find reasons to criticise the Church, but also numerous reasons to defend her.*

Vows at Montmartre

> What is your attitude to the actual, tarnished Church?

36. Home for the Last Time, 1535

NATIVE AIR

By 1535, Ignatius's health began to show serious signs of deterioration. Every fifteen days or so, he would be gripped by terrible stomach pains, followed by a fever. On one occasion, he was overcome by a spasm that lasted sixteen hours. His autopsy revealed gallstones, the cause of these intermittent but extremely painful attacks. When all remedies failed, the doctors finally suggested that there was only one left, namely, that he must breathe the air of his native land.

On this occasion, Ignatius 'let himself be persuaded by his companions', who provided him with additional reasons besides his health for going to Spain. He could visit the families of his Spanish companions and settle business matters in their names. Because of the seriousness of the commitment that he and his companions had made at Montmartre, Ignatius had no qualms about leaving. The group would remain intact. So in the spring of 1535, having been away from home for thirteen years, he found himself making plans to return. He would have the opportunity, he believed, to make amends in Loyola for the bad results of his vanity, his scandalous actions and his pride.

GOOD REPUTATION

As he was about to leave Paris, Ignatius heard alarming news: he had been denounced before the Inquisitor of Paris. So he went on his own to see the Inquisitor and informed him about his impending journey in order that no one could interpret it as flight, and he told him 'that he had companions'. Surely it was because of his concern for his companions that he asked the Inquisitor to hand down a decision on the case. The Inquisitor placed no importance on the charge that had been formally made against him, but expressed an earnest desire to see 'the manuscript of the Exercises'. Having read it, he praised the Exercises highly and asked Ignatius to give him a copy, and this was easily done. Ignatius, not satisfied with the Inquisitor's words of praise, insisted that a judgement on the proceedings be given in proper form. This was done in 1537. When it came to issues of orthodoxy, it is clear that Ignatius was very serious about his reputation.

Before he left Paris, Ignatius paid a visit to a Majorcan student in there. This man, Jerónimo Nadal, confessed to Ignatius that he had been frightened by the prospect of death during a recent illness. He was impressed by the categorical response Ignatius gave him: 'For the past fifteen years I have no longer been afraid of death.' But the little Majorcan had misgivings about the orthodoxy of Ignatius and his group. Though Ignatius tried to dispel all suspicions by outlining for him his future plans, and even told him about persecutions he had undergone at Alcalá and Salamanca, where his innocence had been proven, it was to no avail. The Majorcan, who had a copy of the New Testament in his hand, said farewell to his bothersome sermoniser with these words: 'This is the book I want to follow. I do not know how all of you will end up, and so leave me in peace – for good.' At a later date, Nadal returned to his native Majorca, where he eventually became a canon, but he did not find peace there. Many years afterward, he met Ignatius again in Rome, and in 1545 he became a Jesuit and one of Ignatius's greatest admirers.

HOMEWARD BOUND

Finally, at the end of March 1535, after a stay of seven years in the French capital, the little Basque left Paris, never to return. He said goodbye to his companions and promised to meet them again in Venice. The plan was that they would leave Paris for Venice on the feast of the conversion of Saint Paul, 25 January 1537. This was still a long time off, but Ignatius had confidence that he could leave them in the care of Favre. At this time, the group numbered seven: as yet, no one knew exactly where it was going, but certainly it was headed toward something new. Once more, Ignatius set off alone, but this time not on foot. 'He mounted a small horse which his companions had purchased and he started off alone for his native land, finding himself greatly improved along the way.' The others remained in Paris, finishing their studies.

By returning to Spain, Ignatius was deviating for a moment from his life's journey. He had time as he rode to determine how he should act once he reached his destination. Why not arrive *incognito* and stay, like a typical beggar, in a hospice in his own town of Azpeitia? But his brother got wind of the fact that he was on his way home, and intervened in his plans. Two armed men first passed him by and then followed him in great haste. For once, he confessed, 'he felt a moment of fear'. In such a situation, there is nothing like engaging the individuals in conversation. This is precisely what Ignatius did, and as a result he learned that the two men were servants of his brother, sent to find him. He managed to persuade them to go back to Loyola without him.

In 1595, the illegitimate daughter of Ignatius's brother, Don Pedro, the priest, would remember another adventure of Ignatius on this journey. At

Ignatius's 'great thoughts' of bygone times had not in any way diminished in their intensity; their focus, however, had been changed substantially.

nightfall, he took refuge at an inn, which was a stopover point in this vast open country. The innkeeper did not recognise his guest, but he did speak about him to another guest. This man turned out to be Ignatius's foster-brother. He and the innkeeper peeked through the planks of the door of Ignatius's room and spied on the mysterious traveller. They saw him on his knees, praying in the middle of the room, and the merchant recognised him as Ignatius. He went back straightaway to give the good news to the Loyola family. But Ignatius by-passed the Loyola manor and went to stay in the hospice of the Magdalena in Azpeitia. He was now breathing the spring air of his native land, air he had not breathed since the springtime of 1522. As for the town, it would breathe in a new Ignatius, no longer the young dashing knight so full of energy, but, rather, a wasted, sick and disarmed man. His 'great thoughts' of bygone times had not in any way diminished in their intensity; their focus, however, had been changed substantially.

How has the idealism of your earlier years survived the changes in your life?

Going home to Loyola

37. Beggar and Catechist, 1535

STRANGE BEGGAR

The sober account that Ignatius gives us of his return to Loyola in no way tells us anything about the commotion it provoked in Azpeitia. 'And so he went to the hospice and later, at a convenient time, went out begging for alms in the neighbourhood. In this hospice he began to speak of the things of God with many people who came to visit him, and with God's grace much good was achieved. As soon as he arrived, he determined to teach Christian doctrine every day to the children, but his brother roundly objected to this idea, saying that nobody would come to listen to him. He answered that one would be enough. But after he began his catechism classes, there were many who came faithfully to listen to him, and among them was his brother.' All of this is true, of course, but his account is merely a résumé of the events that transpired.

In the declarations in preparation for Ignatius's beatification, taken sixty years after these events, one can still hear the living echo of Ignatius's footsteps walking through his native land. A considerable number of witnesses both saw and heard Ignatius. Many of them were between ten and fifteen years old at the time. With insatiable curiosity, they surrounded the strange beggar about whom the adults were talking so much. When we put together the bits and pieces that were rescued from popular memory, we can reconstruct this chapter of Ignatius's life, right down to details that we would never expect to find. A twelve-year-old girl who was a servant in the hospice stated that Ignatius first arrived on a Friday afternoon at 5 o'clock. She added that one day she discovered his hair shirt and penitential waist-chains. Some witnesses testified that his family brought a bed from Loyola to the hospice but that Ignatius refused to use it. His family did not think it seemly that a Loyola should live with beggars in a hospice, and they felt it was even less appropriate that, from the very first day he arrived in town, a Loyola should go around begging from door to door for his daily fare. His physical appearance was still very much alive in the memories of these witnesses. He dressed poorly in a dark-brown serge and had sandals made of hemp, which he sometimes tucked into his belt.

The day after his arrival in early April 1535, he began begging. Given his status, his begging brought about a miraculous increase of alms, and some people even began sending gifts to the hospice. Ignatius gave everything he received to the poor at whose table he ate. An old man described how Ignatius apologised for his actions to his brother, but told him that he had not come to Azpeitia to ask anything from the house of Loyola, nor to live in palaces, but rather to sow the Word of God. Next to begging, preaching the Word of God would be his principal activity.

CATECHIST

The regular place for Ignatius's meetings was the hospice church. But soon it was too small to accommodate those who came, and so he had to preach in the open air. The people crowded in on him, and even climbed trees to get a better view. The grass and shrubbery around the hospice turned brown because they were trodden by the crowds. There were some days when Ignatius preached in the parish church. There he made a public confession to the crowd for stealing some fruit during his adolescent years, a theft that had resulted in an innocent person being heavily fined. He explained the Commandments, and every witness remembered his zeal and fervour, and how, despite his reedy voice, the effectiveness and power of what he said could be heard even by those standing far away. Some witnesses recalled that at times he would use strange words that they, as children, only partly understood. One remembered her mother talking about 'the three powers of the soul: the memory, the understanding, and the will'. Another never forgot the emphasis Ignatius placed on the second and sixth Commandments. He condemned concubinage because it could destroy marriage. He helped to patch up broken unions and would summon the absent husband back by writing him a letter. He also helped to make peace between parents and children.

LIFE-CHANGES

Very soon, the effects of Ignatius's preaching could be seen in the moral lives of the people. Blasphemy diminished, people gave up playing cards and gambling, and many who had been leading evil lives amended their ways. The conversion of three prostitutes, whose names were clearly remembered sixty years later, was a particularly important example of his influence. A cousin of one of them remembered the words she heard from the mouth of the most famous of these three: 'Ignatius's words have rent my heart. I have been serving the world; now I want to serve God.' Two of these converted women went on a pilgrimage to Rome: one died on the way. The third did not dare make the pilgrimage because of her age, and instead became a hermit. One witness declared: 'Ignatius achieved what he wanted to do with everyone.' This seems a good description of his powers of persuasion.

Ignatius's most frequent activity and one he always considered important was the humblest of all, that is, teaching children their catechism. One witness stated what a joy it was for her to have learned her catechism from Ignatius. He taught the children how to pray, awakened in them religious sentiments, and explained the Commandments to them. He taught adults too, and his pupils were usually well-behaved. One of these, however, had an ugly, irregular face, and people were always laughing at him. Their laughter hurt Ignatius deeply, partly because this man was a son of the woman who had nursed him, and, like his father before him, was a blacksmith. Ignatius praised him before them all and predicted that one day he would be a great man. Perhaps these words relieved this pupil from the mocking that can prevent people from becoming what they would like to be. At any rate, a desire to become a priest took root in the heart of this blacksmith, and in time he became an outstanding confessor. We can never predict the consequences of a word uttered in a kindly, opportune way.

Ignatius had not come to ask anything from the house of Loyola, nor to live in palaces, but rather to sow the Word of God.

Can you recall the consequences of any words spoken to you in a kindly, considerate way?

38. A Harvest of Good Deeds, 1535

VENERATION

The popular reaction in Azpeitia to Ignatius gradually changed from curiosity to veneration. He was able to calm an epileptic who lived in the hospice, and people considered this miraculous. A woman from a coastal town who had a lung disease also came to see him, and, when she left, she said that she was feeling better. One day some people brought him a young girl who was thought to be possessed. Ignatius advised these people that he did not 'read the Mass' – for he was not yet a priest – but that he would make the sign of the cross over her and pray for her. Although he was not ordained himself, the priests and clerics of the area were his special targets. The force of his personal holiness and his exemplary life, plus the fact that his brother held the patronage over the parish church of Azpeitia, helped him to put some order into their manner of living. They accepted his rule of life, according to one witness, 'as if he had been a bishop or an appointed judge'. He oversaw another agreement which ended an old controversy between the Franciscan nuns and the leading faction at the church. At his suggestion, the people reintroduced the old devotion of praying for the souls in purgatory whenever the church bells rang. He introduced the custom of having the church bells ring at noon, inviting all to pray for those living in mortal sin. The Loyola family perpetuated this custom and gave an annual sum of money to ensure its continuance. One witness saw in this decision on the part of the Loyola family a kind of compensation for the heritage that would have rightfully belonged to Ignatius.

Ignatius's most lasting work was his organisation of public and ordinary assistance for the poor and needy. Laws to this effect were approved by the town council on 23 May 1535. They were designed to stamp out begging and, at the same time, to assist those among the genuinely poor who were ashamed to beg. It is paradoxical that he, the most confirmed beggar in all of Europe, wanted to stamp out begging, but he did so only in the context of providing other support for the poor. In taking this stand, he allied himself with the leaders of the fight against poverty whom he had met in Flanders.

VISITING HOME

During his three months in Azpeitia, Ignatius was too active to have time to think a great deal about his health. We know that apart from his ordinary ailments, he had some serious bouts of illness. Once when he was ill, he was visited and cared for by his nieces, but he had already told his family that he did not come back to Azpeitia to visit the manor house, and, despite pressure, he paid a visit there only once, apart from the day he left for the last time. A witness who was twelve years old at the time remembered the scene vividly. His sister-in-law, accompanied by other members of the family, came to the hospice one day and begged Ignatius to come home for a visit. He said that he was tired and that he would go some other day. She continued her pleading and added that he should do so 'for the sake of your parents' souls'. She then threw herself on her knees and begged him 'through the Passion of Christ' to comply with her request. Ignatius answered: 'You speak to me of the Passion of Christ? For the Passion of Christ I will go not only to Loyola but even to Vergara.' Vergara is about thirty miles from Loyola, and to get there one has to cross a number of difficult mountain ranges. He went to the Loyola manor house at night, but did not sleep there, and was back at the hospice the next morning.

It was not out of any family pressure or because of blood ties that Ignatius made this visit, but to accomplish a daring spiritual mission. He was told that one of his family – probably his brother Martín – was living in concubinage and that every night the woman made her way into the manor house through a secret entrance. Ignatius waited for her, came face to face with her, and asked: 'What are you doing here?' She explained the situation to him. He took her inside and installed her in the room set aside for him: there he kept watch over her until the morning so that she would not sin. When morning came, he put her outside as soon as possible. He had undertaken this desperate action in order to bring the sin of his brother into the light and also to show compassion for his beloved sister-in-law. This was the last sermon he preached, not so much in words as in action, in the manor house.

In later years, Ignatius told this story to another Jesuit. When he came to the part, 'I took her to my own room', the other replied, 'I wouldn't have done that.' 'I did,' Ignatius responded, 'because I knew perfectly well that I could do it.' Then, suddenly realising what he had said, he turned around immediately and said, 'May God forgive you because you made me say something I had no intention of telling.'

ALONE AND ON FOOT

Ignatius's legacy to Azpeitia was a halo of deeds, both praiseworthy and spiritually fruitful, that would be remembered for a long time to come. Many

Many people begged Ignatius to remain, but he told them that 'unless he left he could not serve God as he should and could'.

people begged him to remain, but he told them that 'unless he left he could not serve God as he should and could'. So, despite his brother's entreaties, he made his way toward Pamplona *alone and on foot*.

He also left behind a little pony that he had used. His fellow-countrymen showed their respect and veneration for Ignatius by granting privileges to the pony. In 1552, a Jesuit from Navarre wrote to Ignatius telling him that he had visited the small hospice where Ignatius had stayed. 'We saw the same pony, Father, that you left at the hospice seventeen years ago. It is now very fat and gentle and it serves the hospice well. It enjoys a privileged role in Azpeitia, for whenever it goes into the grain fields, the people look the other way.'

Recall when you have had to leave something good in order to serve God in a new way.

39. From Loyola to Venice, 1535

SPANISH ROADS

When Ignatius left Loyola for the last time, alone and on foot, he set out for a four-month walking journey, which began in the native land of Francis Xavier. There Ignatius delivered to Francis's brother a letter that Francis had written in Paris, which tried to counteract ill feelings that his brother had developed in regard to Ignatius 'as a result of reports given him by certain wretched and contemptible'. Xavier's letter contains the warmest praises of Ignatius, not only because of the 'many times he has assisted me in my needs with money and friends', but also 'because he has been the reason why I gave up evil companions whom I, in my lack of experience, did not recognise as such'. The fact was, the letter continued, that Ignatius was 'a great man of God', and his good way of life was exemplary for all to see. Francis advised his brother that 'your Grace can learn more about my needs and burdens from him than from any other person in the world, since he knows better than anyone else on earth my miseries and needs'. He asked his brother to receive Ignatius 'as you would my own self'.

Ignatius then walked on to Almazán, the home town of Laínez. He then went to Madrid and visited his friend, the governess to Prince Philip. In Toledo, he visited the family of Salmerón. 'But in none of these places would he take anything for himself.' His efforts to regroup the original three companions from Alcalá, and the first group that he had formed in Paris, were to no avail. 'None of them was prepared to follow him,' he noted. He then went to the Carthusian monastery near Segorbe, where he remained for eight days and made a vivid impression on the monks. While there, he spoke with one of his former retreatants and told him about the plans he and his Paris companions had made concerning the future.

NEAR DEATH

So concluded Ignatius's Spanish journey. His immediate plan now was to go on to Italy, where he would pursue his theological studies until he met up in Venice with his companions. Many people attempted to discourage him from making the trip by sea, because the Turkish pirate Barbarossa was all the time menacing the coast of Valencia. 'But although they told him enough to frighten him, nothing they said made him hesitate.' During the crossing from

Valencia to Genoa, the ship lost its rudder in a frightful storm, causing all on board to think that there was no way they were going to escape death. Ignatius did not let this opportunity pass without making a keen observation of his reaction as he came face to face with death. He had told us nothing about his thoughts on death when he confronted it at Pamplona and at Loyola. At Manresa, he had flattered himself by thinking that he was a saint, but, recognising this as a temptation, he had begged those who had come to see him that if, in the future, they found him in such a state, they should cry out and remind him that he was a sinner. During this storm, he notes that he went back over his past life carefully and had no fear because of his sins, only confusion and sorrow for not having made better use of the gifts that the Lord had given him. When, in 1550, he again believed he was going to die, the very thought brought him so much joy and consolation that he had to put it aside as being indicative of selfishness. His changing attitudes toward death reflect his steady spiritual development.

No sooner had he arrived in Genoa than he took off for Bologna, very probably to register at the University. It was the thick of winter and the journey was most difficult. The days were short; the roads had been turned into quagmires and it was bitterly cold. The path he followed through the Apennine mountains hugged a cliff along a river bank. The river was swollen, and the further he went, the higher and narrower the path became. Crawling along on his hands and knees and clutching at the bushes, he came to a point where he was unable either to turn back or to move forward. This time he admitted that he had 'great fear'. Every time he moved he thought he would fall into the river. 'This was indeed the greatest physical strain and exertion that he had ever experienced, but in the end he made it.'

MISHAP IN BOLOGNA

Just as he was crossing over a small wooden bridge in Bologna, he fell into a creek and came out of it soaked to the bone and covered with sludge. 'The people who were watching, and there were many there, had a good laugh.' This was his introduction to some very difficult days ahead. He went through the whole town begging, but did not get a single coin nor even a crust of bread. Eventually, he encountered some former acquaintances, and he was able to dry out his clothes and refresh himself. At first he thought he could study in Bologna and he went so far as to get some money from his Catalan friend, Isabel Roser. But he could not endure Bologna's cold, heavy fog. He was confined to bed for eight days in December 1535 with chills, fever and his old companion, stomach cramps. By this date, he had already developed his Christian theory of sickness, which he had shared with Isabel Roser in a letter dated 1532. God uses sickness and infirmities, he said, 'to show us the shortness of this life'. He continued: 'And when I think that he visits those whom he loves through these infirmities, I can feel no sadness or pain, because I believe a servant of God who goes through a sickness comes out of it already half a doctor, because he can straighten out and order his life for the glory and service of God.'

Without picking up any more academic diplomas, but half-way through his course work for a doctorate in virtue, he departed for Venice toward the end of December 1535, where he soon felt much better. He still had a long year – the whole of 1536 – before the agreed date when he would meet with his companions.

Ignatius's changing attitudes toward death reflect the successive spiritual states he had come to know.

Between Valencia and Genoa

Reflecting on times when you were sick, can you notice what good came out of them?

40. Exercises and Study in Venice, 1536

A QUIET YEAR

The year 1536 was a relatively calm year in Ignatius's life, and his health seemed to improve. In Venice, he had time to study theology, but on his own, because there was not a single university in that extraordinary city. He did not have to make so many trips and excursions, and his accommodation was provided by 'a very good and erudite man', who may have been the Spanish Consul, whom Ignatius described in a letter written in 1540 as 'an old friend and brother in the Lord'. The alms he received regularly that year from Isabel Roser in Barcelona, and from friends in Paris, freed him from being a burden on anyone and from having to beg for his food. Consequently, he felt no anxiety, no pressure, during this year's stay in Venice.

While there, he was invited by an old Barcelona friend to preach a series of Lenten sermons in Barcelona itself. In his answer, Ignatius said that although he desired to meet the needs of the city to which he owed more 'than to any other city in the world', he preferred 'to preach in a minor capacity, like a poor man, on subjects that are more easily understood and of less importance'. He added that as soon as he finished his studies he was going to send Isabel Roser his books. In a letter to a Paris benefactor, he stated: 'I enjoy perfect bodily health and I await the coming of Lent so that I can put aside my studies and concentrate on things of greater importance, duration, and value.'

LETTERS

Ignatius did not dedicate his time in Venice exclusively to quiet study. It was here that the solitary Ignatius took up letter-writing, and some of these Venice letters are particularly rich in doctrinal matters, such as the two he addressed to Sister Teresa Rajadell, a Benedictine nun in Barcelona. These letters give very precise rules for prayer and the discernment of spirits and, when we read between the lines, they teach us a great deal about Ignatius's own experience. He frequently spoke in these Venice letters about the trials that affected others and he showed himself to be much more sensitive than one might suspect to the problems of those around him. He did not lend his voice publicly to the critical spirits of the age, and he did not consider as a true Christian anyone who, in pointing out vices within the Church, caused the

Church to suffer. Yet his love for the Church, 'the true spouse of Jesus Christ', did not blind him from recognising abuses within the Church.

It was from Venice in 1536 that Ignatius wrote a very personal letter to his old friend and confessor, Dr Miona, who had helped him at Alcalá and later in Paris. Miona still had some misgivings about Ignatius's future, and had put off making the Exercises. Ignatius begged him to take the step immediately. 'I ask you to do what I have already requested of you, knowing as I do that the Exercises are the best means I can think of in this life by which persons can both benefit themselves and bring help, profit and advantage to many others. Even though you feel yourself in no special need, you will see how they will help you to serve others beyond anything you have ever dreamed of.' Miona eventually did what Ignatius requested, and as a result he entered the Society of Jesus in 1545.

THE EXERCISES

Ignatius also busied himself with organising a programme whereby spiritual conversations could occur. These gatherings were more than simply pious get-togethers. His preferred task, however, was to give the Spiritual Exercises. To paraphrase the beginning of the First Letter of Saint John, he was not able to keep silent about what he had seen with his own eyes and touched with his own hands, namely, the Word Incarnate. He was not selling a programme for self-control or equanimity. He wanted to go to the root of a person's destiny, and he helped many to see for themselves what their destiny was. He wanted people to be able to approach God and the world with an attitude of gratitude and service. This was the 'Principle and Foundation' upon which his Exercises were built.

Ignatius gives us the names of distinguished persons who made these Exercises. To one, he later wrote: 'If you have possessions [his correspondent belonged to a very wealthy family] they should not possess you, nor should you be possessed by anything temporal.' This had become Ignatius's motto, and it had grown more out of his own personal experience than from some theoretical principle, because, as he confessed, he savoured more each day what Saint Paul had written: 'Yet here we are, having nothing and yet owning everything' (1 Corinthians 6:2). A cleric named Hoces from Malaga, who was both well educated and virtuous, had had a desire to make the Exercises, but had never put his good intentions into execution. At last he did so, and on the third day of his retreat he made a surprising confession to Ignatius: he had been frightened into thinking that in making the Exercises he might be taught some wrong doctrine, and he had come armed with books which he hoped would guard him against deception. This attitude came as a result of what 'someone else had told him'.

'The Exercises are the best means I can think of in this life by which persons can both benefit themselves and bring help, profit and advantage to many others.'

It is all but absolutely certain that the one who had sowed this doubt in his soul was Bishop Carafa, who was destined to be named a cardinal in a short time, and a few years later would be elected Pope Paul IV. Hoces profited to such an extent from the Exercises that, as happened with Ignatius's companions in Paris, he expressed the wish 'to follow the pilgrim's manner of life'.

Reflect on the steps you have taken over the years to develop your spiritual life.

41. Disagreement with a Future Pope, 1536

REFORMED PRIESTS?

Bishop Carafa became Pope Paul IV in 1554. Events in 1536 show that he and Ignatius were mutually repellent personalities. Even though both had the same goal, which was to establish a group of 'reformed priests' to help the Church, their methods of dealing with people were very different indeed. What the bishop had done in regard to Hoces was insidious and, from an objective point of view, slanderous. He had implanted in the heart of a retreatant of Ignatius a deep suspicion of Ignatius's orthodoxy and even attempted to feed these suspicions as time went on. Ignatius and the bishop had met face to face and their conversation had revolved around the reformed priests – called Theatines – who were under Carafa's jurisdiction. They discussed the topic in depth, and it would not be hazardous to suggest that Carafa gave way to a fit of anger, which, as pope twenty years later, he was still not able to hide.

We know Ignatius's viewpoints because of a letter he sent to Carafa. He did not seem concerned whether the letter was well thought-out or not. With startling simplicity, he requested, as a lay man standing before a bishop, that his letter be received with the same affection, good will and sincerity with which it had been written. He began with an undeniable fact regarding the feeble growth of the company of the Theatines founded by Carafa in 1524. And 'as the little ones do ordinarily before the great', he dared to give what he thought were the reasons why the group had not increased. The first cause was the style of life of Carafa himself. Ignatius said that he personally was not scandalised that the person who was the leader of the group had better clothes, because his dignity as a bishop and his advanced years demanded it. On the other hand, he believed 'it would have been the part of wisdom to call to mind' the examples of older models, like Francis of Assisi and Dominic, and the way that they had given example to their followers. Instead of indulging in weakness, the leader should give an example of leading his companions in virtue. A considerable amount of autobiographical material is expressed by Ignatius in this principle.

Next, Ignatius examined the style of Carafa's new Congregation. The Theatines, he said, were too concentrated on the internal life of the group itself; they were addicted to the singing of the divine office; they depended on alms, and yet they did not go out and preach nor did they practise the corporal works of mercy or undergo the humiliation of having to beg. Ignatius did not dare to put in writing other matters that were of even greater importance. From this negative description of the Theatines, we can deduce the positive ideal of a religious order that he himself had at this period of his life.

SEASONED HEROES

Ignatius's criticism of Carafa, as harsh as it was frank, had the effect of producing an open break between these two leaders, and when Carafa was made a cardinal and came to Rome, Ignatius would have to suffer the consequences of his naked animosity. Ignatius never revealed any of the details of his face-to-face meeting with Carafa, at which time he not only criticised the other's ideas, but also laid bare his own most personal convictions. In his view, only heroic exploits really seize people and produce life. Ignatius's dreams were of seasoned heroes and not of monks installed in the heart of a city. Thanks to the group that he had left behind in Paris, and would meet again in a year's time, his dream would soon become a reality.

The small group of select men whom Ignatius had left in Paris lived up to his expectations. His departure for Spain to recuperate had saddened them, but the group was solid enough for them to stick together and it could almost have gone on without him. All had been dedicating themselves wholeheartedly to their studies, and at the same time they continued confessing and receiving Holy Communion weekly and kept up their practice of daily meditation. Their intimate friendship with one another bound them together and was a great support to each one. After all, what ultimately kept them together was Christ, not Ignatius. This was the reason why, despite Ignatius's absence, they had renewed in 1535 and 1536 the vow they had taken together at Montmartre on 15 August 1534.

NEW COMPANIONS

The group had also had the satisfaction of seeing three additional companions join, all from France. Two, Jay and Broët, were already priests. They had got to know the original companions through Pierre Favre, who up until then had been the only ordained priest. Favre was the head of the group, not as a superior nor as a second Ignatius, but simply as the one who was senior among the companions. The cohesiveness of the group came about from the fact that all of them lived out the Exercises. Favre showed a great mastery in using this Ignatian method with others. He also had a special grace for the ministry of the confessional and a real gift of sympathy, which attracted many people to him. One of his numerous penitents was the seventeen-year-old Portuguese named Luis Gonçalves da Câmara, to whom Ignatius would dictate his *Autobiography* between 1553 and 1555.

On 3 October 1536, while Ignatius was in Venice, Favre, Rodrigues, Salmerón, Bobadilla, Jay, Codure and Broët were given their Master of Arts degrees. Laínez and Francis Xavier had already received theirs. However, these two were not able to obtain the degree of Master of Theology because this would take many more years, and the date for their departure from Paris, 27 January 1537, was fast approaching. In fact, they had to move this date back to the November of 1536 because of the fresh war between France and Spain. Before leaving Paris, Laínez and Xavier did manage to get a parchment attesting that they had studied theology in the Theological Faculty of Paris for one-and-a-half years.

In Ignatius's view, only heroic exploits really seize people and produce life.

Waiting for God

Have you found yourself seized over the years by the heroic exploits of others?

42. From Paris to Venice, 1536-37

HERETICS?

The abrupt interruption by Ignatius's group of their studies and their apostolic works, and their sudden departure from Paris, was a cause of surprise to many. One of the doctors of the University put a case of conscience before Favre, which was certainly not altogether far-fetched. He argued that the group was unquestionably doing good in Paris: now the companions were risking this certain good for a project based on idle fancy. Was it therefore possible that they were committing a mortal sin by leaving Paris? The doctor even asked Favre's permission to submit this case to the doctors at the theological faculty. But the companions were firm in their decision, and did not need the protection of high-placed persons whom Ignatius had recommended to them in case of need. However, their sudden disappearance from Paris did indeed resemble a flight, and a few years later, while they were in Italy, the accusation was made that they had hurried away from Paris in the same way as many heretics had already done.

WINTER WALKING

Rodrigues records the adventures and perils of their journey to Venice. To avoid travelling through war-zones, they decided on a longer and more difficult itinerary, which took them eventually through Germany and then over the Alps. Some of the companions set out five or six days before the others, who delayed to distribute to the poor all the group's possessions. It is probable that this last contingent left Paris on 15 November before daybreak, so that they would not be noticed. At the end of the first day's walking, they met with a group of peasants and soldiers, who asked who they were, where they were coming from and where were they going. The French companions answered, in the name of the whole group, that they were students from Paris. But were they monks or priests? At this point, a little old lady interrupted the soldiers: 'Oh, leave them alone,' she said, 'they are going off to reform some province.' With that, everyone laughed heartily and the crowd let them continue on their way.

From that moment on, they decided that, while in France, only the French companions would answer questions; the Spaniards would confine their speech to saying that they were students from Paris. This unchanging and vague answer once prompted a soldier who was interrogating them to call one of the Spaniards 'a dumb ox'. They were, of course, dressed in the long gowns that students wore; moreover, they wore broad-brimmed hats and each carried a pilgrim's staff. All of them had leather wallets suspended from their shoulders, and in these they carried their Bibles, breviaries and papers, and each had a rosary that hung openly from around his neck. To facilitate walking, they picked up their gowns and tucked them into their belts. When Rodrigues reminisced about these events forty years later, he recalled vividly the immense trust and confidence each of the companions had in God, and the extraordinary happiness that was theirs. They were undertaking such a joyful celebration that it seemed to them that their feet never touched the ground. The two groups met at a town twenty-eight miles east of Paris, where they determined that they would stay together until they had completed their journey. Rather than begging on the way, they would use what money they had until they arrived in Venice. They prayed, meditated, sang hymns and recited the divine office along the way. If asked where they were going, they would answer that they were on pilgrimage to a sanctuary in Lorraine. It rained constantly in France and by the time they got to Germany snow was falling. 'We were novices at walking,' observed Laínez. Most probably, they came to have the greatest admiration for the vigour shown by Ignatius, who was a professional hiker.

ALONG THE WAY

Various incidents enlivened their itinerary. At one time, Rodrigues became separated from the rest and, as a result, he had to put up a vigorous fight with a peasant who was intent on bringing him 'to visit a very beautiful girl'. When they reached Germany, the Spaniards did the talking for the whole group, saying that they were students from Paris on their way to make a pilgrimage at Loreto: this meant that sometimes they had to swallow taunts from the Protestants. If the cold and snow were the pincers that tore at their bodies, face-to-face contact with real live Protestants racked their souls. Tired and worn out by exposure, they finally arrived in Basel, where they recuperated from their exertions for three days and defended the tenets of the Catholic faith. Then they started out again, this time for Constance, about a hundred miles from Basel. But because they knew neither German nor the local dialect and roads, they lost their way a number of times.

On one such occasion, they stumbled into a Protestant village. It was night, and the people were celebrating the wedding of the local parish priest with music, eating, drinking and dancing. In another town, the married priest lost a debate with them and threatened to have them thrown into prison. After a terrifying night, during which they thought that they were surely going to die,

Rodrigues recalled vividly the immense trust and confidence each of the companions had in God, and the extraordinary happiness that was theirs.

a young man who sympathised with them managed to help them escape before daybreak. In Constance, which was a thoroughly Protestant town, they were able with difficulty to celebrate Mass in a small church before a congregation that had to pay a tax for the privilege. Just before they entered Lindau, an old woman approached them from a leper hospital, shouting with emotion and trying to kiss the rosaries that hung from around their necks. Then she showed them heads and hands that the heretics had lopped off from statues of the saints and that she had wisely kept. Later, she accompanied them to the gates of the city, crying out to bystanders: 'See here, you cheats and frauds! Here are true Christian men. Did not all of you tell me, you lying frauds, that everyone had embraced the errors of the heretics? You lied. Now I know you for what you are, and so you will not fool me again!' Neither threats nor favours had been able to tear away the ancient faith from this non-conforming old woman.

Recall some difficult moments when you were surprised to experience great trust and happiness in God.

43. From Venice to Rome, 1537

HOSPITAL WORK

On 8 January 1537, Ignatius's companions arrived in Venice. Their meeting with Ignatius there was the cause of tremendous joy to all, and they introduced him to their three new companions. He, too, had some companions to introduce to them. The group had two months to wait before going to Rome for papal permission to travel to the Holy Land, so Ignatius arranged for them to work in two hospitals in the meantime. The immersion of these university scholars into the Venetian hospitals of the time, performing most unpleasant tasks, must have been a brutal experience, and they needed gigantic inner resources to take them on. To overcome his natural revulsion to the sores of a syphilitic patient, Xavier forced himself to lick these lesions. As for Rodrigues, when he learned that a leper had been denied a bed in the hospital, he invited the man to share his own bed. Later on, Xavier thought that he had become infected with syphilis as a result of his action, and Rodrigues was sick for a whole day out of fear that he had contracted leprosy.

STARVING BEGGARS

After two months of trials in the hospitals, the companions went as a group to Rome to ask for the pope's blessing on their Jerusalem venture. Ignatius, however, did not go with them. His decision was a discreet, cautionary measure. He wanted to stay clear both of the newly created Cardinal Carafa with whom he had difficulties a short time ago, and of Doctor Ortiz, who had denounced him to the Inquisitor in Paris, and was now in Rome. Perhaps Ignatius also wanted his group to suffer the trials of making a pilgrimage devoid of his company. Unlike the trip that they had made from Paris to Venice, this time the companions made the journey in abject poverty, living on alms alone. We know that they arrived in Ravenna soaked to the skin, exhausted, and half-dead with hunger. They were accustomed to travelling in groups of three, with a priest assigned to each group, and they followed Ignatius's example by spending the night in hospices, hay lofts and even stables. They ate whatever was given to them, keeping no provisions for the road. On one occasion, they walked the whole day barefoot in the streaming rain, praying and singing psalms, with nothing more in their stomachs than the little bread they had eaten in the early morning. Once, someone mistook them for a group of veteran soldiers who had participated in the sack of Rome in 1527 and were on their way to ask the pope for his forgiveness.

In order to pay ship's passage from Ravenna to Ancona, they had to pawn a breviary. They ate like the destitute. At Ancona, Laínez stood barefoot and politely thanked a woman selling vegetables in a market for giving him a radish, a cabbage and an apple. They stayed in Loreto for three days, giving themselves over to prayer and devotions. At Tolentino, a foreigner gave them a dinner composed of bread, figs and wine, which they shared with other beggars. At last, on Palm Sunday, 25 March 1537, they arrived in Rome, where they were received in their respective national hospices. The previous four months had constituted a tough noviciate. As Laínez later said, during this time they had adopted 'the way of life' of Ignatius, which meant leaving the things of this world and placing their trust in God alone. Those months had been for them the most heroic period of their lives.

PAPAL WELCOME

Meanwhile, the situation had changed in Rome in the most unexpected way imaginable. The redoubtable Doctor Ortiz, who had denounced Ignatius in Paris, had become his most solid defender, and he even obtained an audience for the group with Pope Paul III. And what an audience it was! Ortiz told the pope about these nine most promising Paris theologians who wanted to travel in total poverty to Jerusalem. Their story was most unusual, almost miraculous. Paul III liked to be surrounded by newcomers to Rome who gave promise of livening up his meals, and so he invited them to dine with him, during the course of which he listened to the philosophical and theological disputations they engaged in with other invited theologians. These Paris masters, who only a few days back were sleeping in stables, had now taken their places alongside cardinals and learned doctors at the table of the pope. Paul III was charmed by them, and, following the custom, he asked them what it was that they desired. They said that they wanted neither money nor ecclesiastical appointment, but only his permission to go to Jerusalem. In a formal document, permission was bestowed upon Favre and twelve companions to visit and remain in the Holy Land and to return whenever it pleased them to do so. This specification of privileges would offset any pressure from the Franciscan Guardian to depart, as he had ordered Ignatius to do in 1523. The vow that they had made at Montmartre in 1534 was being scrupulously followed.

OPEN DOORS

The pope and cardinals had collected two hundred and sixty ducats to assist the companions in making their voyage to the Holy Land. Moreover, the pope gave the priests among them the power, usually reserved to bishops, to absolve certain serious sins. Those who were not yet priests were given permission to receive Holy Orders, including the priesthood, from the hands of any bishop, and without observing the prescribed canonical delays. And so these strange pilgrims returned to Venice begging, but in their shoulder bags, the hallmarks of beggars and mendicant monks, they were carrying more concessions than they could ever have dreamed possible. Of all of these various privileges, the most surprising was the open door to the priesthood. They were not tied to a particular diocese, and could be ordained 'under the title of voluntary poverty and sufficient learning'. In July of that same year, 1537, Ignatius commented on all of these special privileges: the companions, he wrote, 'living in penury, without money, without recommendations ... but putting all their confidence in God ... obtained, without any effort on their part, *much more than what they had sought....*'. They had, after all, only asked permission to go to the Holy Land! Such was the experience of these 'nine friends in the Lord', which was the expression Ignatius used when referring to the companions who had come from Paris. Two more recently recruited companions failed to show sufficient tenacity and strength of character and eventually left the group, though one would cause them trouble later.

'Putting all their confidence in God, they obtained, without any effort on their part, much more than they had sought ...'

Recall times when you put your confidence in God and obtained more than you had sought.

44. Venice and Vicenza, 1537

IGNATIUS ORDAINED

After their return from Rome to Venice, the companions went back to their regular hospital jobs. Bobadilla, Laínez, Xavier, Codure, Rodrigues and Ignatius himself were ordained priests in Venice on 24 June 1537, the feast of Saint John the Baptist. Salmerón was ordained a deacon, but because of his youth he had to wait until the following June to be ordained a priest. The papal legate in Venice gave them all the faculties they needed to carry out their ministry in the territory that he governed, without permission of the local bishop. At long last, Ignatius, along with the others, was empowered to determine 'when it was a question of a mortal or venial sin', because now he was able to hear confessions, grant absolution in reserved cases, dispense the sacraments, preach, and give lectures on holy Scripture. After fifteen years, the restrictions placed on him by the Inquisition in Alcalá and Salamanca were no longer binding. The companions were now known as 'reformed priests' – that is, of sound morals and doctrine, unlike many priests of those times. It goes without saying that these 'friends in the Lord' dreamed of saying their first Masses in the land of Jesus. Everything – and even more than everything – that they had planned in Paris in 1534 had become a reality, except the most important of all, the journey to Jerusalem.

JERUSALEM?

For the first time in forty years, the pilgrim ships were not able to weigh anchor for the Holy Land because a formidable Turkish armada was threatening the Venetian fortresses and islands along the Adriatic. All possibilities for peace seemed totally exhausted, and, as we read in the *Autobiography*, Ignatius and his companions 'saw their hopes diminishing' as far as going to the Holy Land was concerned. Ignatius was used to dealing with unforeseeable situations and so, at first, he and his companions did not give up hope; rather, they determined to spend twelve whole months in Venice, that is, all the rest of 1537, up to the summer of 1538. During this time of waiting, they would spread themselves throughout the Venetian possessions. Accordingly, they drew lots to determine the make-up of teams of two or three, but before doing this they sent back to Rome two hundred ducats, the money they had not already used from the alms they had received in April. Now, toward the end of July, they were ready to give themselves unreservedly to the demanding service of hospital work, but first they would set aside a few months to live hidden, solitary lives, free from all commitments, during which time they could prepare themselves for the day when they would offer their first Masses.

BOILED BREAD

Ignatius, Favre and Laínez went to Vicenza, where they took lodgings on the outskirts of the town in a small house that had been let to them by local monks. This house was almost totally in ruins, having neither doors nor windows. They slept on the ground, with a little bit of straw for a bed. At this time of his life, Ignatius was already accustomed to weeping easily and frequently; his eyes were sunken and he was highly sensitive to both light and wind. For this reason, it was Favre and Laínez who went into town twice a day to beg, but what they brought back was never sufficient to satisfy their hunger. Ignatius, since he normally stayed at home, was the cook, although usually what he prepared were crusts of bread, which he boiled in order to make them edible. Whenever they had a bit of oil or lard, it was a veritable feast. They spent forty days living this type of penitential life, totally cut off from everyone, 'intent on nothing but their prayers'. The way they had opted to live in Vicenza was an obvious imitation of how Christ had prepared himself for entering his public life, a life they themselves had dreamed of re-enacting in Palestine.

The other teams went through this same forty days in prayer. It was summer, at the height of the dog days, and swarms of mosquitoes distracted their solitude and contributed to their penances. Most certainly, these mosquitoes were also the cause of the fevers that many of the companions suffered. The sickness of Rodrigues was particularly severe. Ignatius, himself hospitalised at the time with fever, was anxious about Rodrigues's welfare, and he went to visit him in Bassano, walking so fast that Favre was not able to keep up with him. When Codure joined the group at Vicenza, Ignatius, Favre and Laínez began to preach in the city squares, shouting loudly to the people and attracting them by waving their large Paris-style academic bonnets. The quality of their Italian was indisputably lower than the force of their simple words.

Little by little, the whole group was reunited in Vicenza, and at this point the local people began to show more generosity towards them. In September 1537, Salmerón was ordained a priest. At the beginning of autumn, Xavier, Laínez, Bobadilla and Codure said their first Masses. These Masses were events of the spirit, celebrated as they were without family, friends or feasting. Ignatius put off saying his first Mass, undoubtedly because he still

Ignatius, since he normally stayed at home, was the cook, although usually what he prepared were crusts of bread, which he boiled in order to make them edible.

cherished the hope of being able to offer it in the land of Jesus.

HOLDING THE SECRET

Ignatius was the father to each of them. Quiet and discreet, he seemed to be the trustee of the secret of the future, and yet this future was also uncertain for him. There was a personal, profound, intimate mystery about him that is not clarified when he tells us that during these months in Vicenza 'he received many spiritual visions and great consolation that was almost continuous ... and he enjoyed great supernatural visitations of the kind he had in Manresa'. We are moved by what he did, his poverty, his cooking for the others, but we know nothing about the plans and dreams simmering in his own heart. Apparently, he led the group democratically: he was by no means the pompous leader, the authoritarian chief, the strategic administrator. He wanted all of them to decide personally how to fulfil the vow they had made at Montmartre.

Have you lived through lean times, and if so, how have they affected you?

45. Friends in the Lord, 1537

WAITING

'All of them will now separate and go to different places in Italy and wait another year for an opportunity to set sail for Jerusalem. If God our Lord does not judge this voyage good for his service, they will not wait any longer, but rather they will continue to pursue what they have already begun.' So wrote Ignatius in a letter to a friend in July 1537. Until the hour of decision arrived, the companions went off in groups of two or three to the university cities, Siena, Ferrara and Padua. They hoped to attract new students to their group. Xavier, accompanied by Bobadilla, went to Bologna, the city where his own father had received a doctorate in 1470. Favre, Ignatius and Laínez would travel to Rome, encouraged by the invitation from Doctor Ortiz, who previously had been so much feared. If the doctor had quelled his own suspicions about the group, new ones were hatched that year in Venice itself. Ignatius with good reason called these suspicions 'persecutions'. It was said that he had been burned in effigy in Spain and in Paris. This rumour meant that he could be considered a heretic on the run. Fortunately, a well-placed friend of Ignatius and one of his former exercitants attested that the accusations against 'a certain priest named Ignatius of Loyola' were frivolous, vain and false. And so for the fifth time, Ignatius saw his orthodoxy confirmed. After this judgement, he was at last able to leave his companions in peace and tranquillity, and this is what he did in the autumn of 1537.

THE COMPANY OF JESUS

What were the companions to say if they were asked who they were? They were friends, companions and equals, co-founders of something still unspecified. They had neither an approved rule nor a legitimate superior. They were friends held together by Jesus Christ and, therefore, when they were asked who they were, they should say that they belonged to the Company of Jesus. The name 'Company' conveyed something more than a confraternity, but something less than a full-fledged order. The name came into being before the actual organisation that would be known in history as the Company, or Society, of Jesus. When all was said and done, the name did nothing more than define this extraordinary group of friends, who identified themselves solely in relation to Christ.

They wanted to follow Jesus, but in the footsteps of Ignatius, as one might do when one places a foot in the imprint left on the snow by someone who has gone ahead. This desire to follow Ignatius explains why the companions continued, as they had done earlier, to visit hospitals and prisons, to go from door to door begging for their food, to teach catechism to children and adults, and to practise giving what they had to the poor. Furthermore, they could and did perform priestly ministry, and they did so gratuitously, in accord with their vow of poverty. The companions travelled together in pairs, and the two were never of the same nationality: they agreed to obey each other, alternating as the superior every other week. Ignatius also obeyed, although they all regarded him with reverence. Not everyone, however, was able to understand this strange type of life that they led. The vicar general at Padua had Codure and Hoces imprisoned and placed in chains in order to put a stop to their activities. Hoces was not able to contain his inner joy, and so he laughed loudly when he found himself behind bars. However, next morning the prelate had a change of heart and released the two companions.

TO ROME

Ignatius had confidence in all his companions and in their sense of personal responsibility, but it was taken for granted that each had to fend for himself. Unexpectedly, toward the end of October 1537, he himself set off for Rome, accompanied by Favre and Laínez. Favre specified that they had been called to the eternal city, although he does not say why nor by whom. Even though the purpose of this trip remains obscure, its results were decisive in focusing some light onto the obscure zones of the companions' collective future.

As they passed through Bologna, Laínez fell desperately ill and was unable to walk. Ignatius rented a horse for him while he himself walked on ahead at such a fast pace that the two younger men were astounded. He had always achieved what he considered was God's will for him. Now, however, a doubt was beginning to gnaw at his soul: was it possible that God would counteract the plan to go to Jerusalem, a plan that all of them had cherished for so many years and that each one of them saw so clearly as being what God was asking each one to do? If ever there was a man who believed completely in divine providence, it was Ignatius – a man, moreover, who let himself be guided by movements of the supernatural – but now he was in the throes of deep confusion, going through a dark night and seeking protection from on high, as he had done in other times of crisis.

LA STORTA

Along the way, not far from the city of Rome, Ignatius entered a tiny chapel that stood alone and abandoned, called La Storta. What actually happened there belongs in the category of those decisive events of his life, and, like Loyola and Manresa, it too became a watershed. Between the lines in his *Autobiography*, we hear but weak vibrations of what was a deep seismic event. 'One day,' he said, 'a few miles before they reached Rome, he was praying in a church and experienced such a change in his soul and saw so clearly that God the Father had placed him with Christ his Son that his mind could not doubt that the Father had indeed placed him with his Son … and he heard our Lord and Redeemer himself say to him: "I will be favourable to you in Rome"'.

If ever there was a man who believed completely in divine providence, it was Ignatius.

How strong is your belief in divine providence, and what experience is it born of?

46. 'I will be favourable to you in Rome', 1537

PLACED WITH THE SON

After Ignatius's death, those who went through his personal effects found the following key phrase among his notes: '*When the Father was placing me with his Son.*' The reference to La Storta is clear, even though in itself the phrase is not particularly enlightening. Ignatius was not the kind of mystic who tortured himself trying to express what was, by definition, inexpressible. He guarded it and kept quiet about it, but it had made a branding-iron impression on him. The vision of La Storta was the final phase of a period that had been rich in visionary phenomena for him. This period included the long retreat he had made during the earlier part of that interminable year of 1537, a year that had become more and more hopeless as the months crawled by. Ignatius had always been a man who regarded even the most insignificant happenings as being heaven-sent, and therefore having to forget his plan to spend the rest of his life in Jerusalem had the effect of reducing him to a state of utter bewilderment.

I will be favourable to you in Rome. I, that is Christ himself, whom he had sought in his dreams about Jerusalem; *I will be favourable*, Christ will be graciously disposed; *to you*, the group of friends – not Ignatius alone – were the object of this reassuring promise; *in Rome*, the direction-sign pointed away from Jerusalem toward Rome, which, ever since their Paris days, had been the companions' alternative plan if they were prevented from travelling to the Holy Land.

ROME, MAGNIFICENT …

After La Storta, Ignatius the pilgrim was convinced that he was travelling in the right direction; however, the road was full of many uncertainties. He had a premonition that difficulties, trials, persecutions – in a word, hostility – awaited them in Rome, and he expressed this premonition with a graphic metaphor: he said he saw ahead 'closed windows and doors'. Certitude and assurance did not mean for him that the road ahead was clearly visible and the horizon cloudless. His only option was to go on walking. The Rome that Ignatius, Favre and Laínez reached in the autumn of 1537 was a complex reality. Countless churches, majestic palaces and grandiose monuments soared over the humble dwellings of the ordinary people. In spite of the fact that Italy was strangled by foreign powers and Protestants were waging terrible attacks against Rome, whose voice was scarcely heeded anymore in many parts of Europe, the city was still energised by the spirit of the Renaissance. Arts and letters were thriving, and even the population showed signs of continued growth. Rome was indeed unique. A new nobility was challenging the power and influence of the dominant families, matching them in ostentation with their new palaces and villas. The glorious past of both pagan and Christian times was present in the ancient monuments that had been at least partially saved from ruin, in the innumerable churches and magnificent fountains, and in the catacombs that were just then being rediscovered.

... BUT CORRUPT

The cardinals in the Curia, or papal administration, with their large following of lackeys and protégés, played an important role in the management of the Catholic world, but also in the battles that took place every time a conclave was called to elect a new pope. The ambassadors of the most important governments brought to the city the heartbeat of the world, and here in Rome they vied to bring glory to the kings and princes they represented by making themselves ever visible and by engaging in all types of disputes. University scholars and clerics from all over Europe flocked to Rome by the hundreds, looking for positions in the Curia, or for living quarters in the palaces of this cardinal or that bishop, or for appointments or salaries. From the days of the Avignon popes, Rome had become a gigantic agency, where appointments to office were handed out, and for this reason it had become the city of intrigue, ambition, greed and graft. Money opened doors. Everything could be bought or sold, irrespective of the fact that the real purpose of the revenue that came from an ecclesiastical office was intended for the pastoral services of the people. Buying and selling Church offices had become the greatest scourge and the most nefarious evil in the Church because, among many other abuses, it was tied to such evils as special privileges, plurality of Church offices, absenteeism and the trading of dioceses and parishes. A contemporary Dominican moralist described the condition of the Church of that time as 'the subversion of order'.

CHURCH REFORM?

In vain had generation after generation of reformers called for action that would cut off these evils at the root, but their complaints either became lost in the void of outer space or were pulverised when they clashed against the gigantic centralising, fiscal machine that was the Roman Curia. The Curia had too much interest in maintaining the *status quo* to support any serious

Rome was the city of intrigue, ambition, greed and graft. Money opened doors. Everything could be bought or sold.

reform. The events that had taken place during the terrible sack of Rome in 1527, when the city was subjected to the atrocities of foreign troops and the pope was imprisoned at Castel Sant'Angelo, were still fresh in the memory of the people, who reacted emotionally to any foreign intervention in Roman institutions. There was no shortage of preachers and prophets who saw in that dreadful time of pillage God's punishment for the many sins of the so-called 'holy city'. Others prophesied – or perhaps just expressed their desire – that an angelic, heaven-sent pope would come along and remedy all the existing evils.

How do you compare the Church of the sixteenth century with the Church of today?

Vision at La Storta

47. Servants of the Pope, 1538

INEFFECTUAL REFORM

Things had not improved much by late 1537 when Ignatius, Favre and Laínez arrived in Rome. The reigning pope was Paul III, a Farnese who had more of the charm of a Renaissance man than the attraction of an angel. He had begun his climb to power under the Borgia pope, Alexander VI, and had managed to accumulate a number of bishoprics on the way. Elected pope in 1534, he consistently showed more concern for the advancement of his family in general and of his two sons in particular than for any effective reform of the Church. However, the renovation he made in the College of Cardinals by bestowing the red hat on certain outstanding men, two of whom would become popes after him, did give cause for hope. Later on, Ignatius and his companions would have dealings with these men and they would be strong allies of the Society. A number of these cardinals put together, in 1536, the famous *Programme for the Reform of the Church*, which pinpointed the ills that called for remedies. The cardinals expressed concern about exaggerated theories of pontifical authority and drew up basic guidelines for reform, which dealt with, among other items, curial accountability, limitation of exemptions, the training of future priests and the improvement of preaching. Their programme was solid and intelligently set forth, a symbol of healthy thinking and good will, but it remained a dead letter.

It is true that Paul III did order bishops living in Rome to return to their own dioceses, but his orders were not carried out. His attempt to call a Council was met with even more conspicuous failure. No one on the Catholic side responded to his appeal, and added to this slight was the outright refusal on the part of Protestants to attend any Council whatsoever. The result was that the hoped-for Council of Trent was not summoned until 1542, and even then the first session had to be postponed until the end of 1545 because of the incessant war between Francis I and Charles V.

SELF-OFFERING

Despite all these obstacles, the spirit of reform was not restricted to the fringes of the Catholic world. It was, rather, more of a hope than the reality of things that animated Catholic thinking at the very heart of the Church. Side by side with the Rome of officialdom was another Rome, that of the ordinary people, who took delight in celebrating the carnival and other festivities, who were despised and humiliated by the aristocrats and who held on to their secular traditions and religious superstitions. There were also many hospitals, innumerable confraternities and charitable organisations that existed cheek by jowl with the corrupt moral life of the city and the many prostitutes in the streets. It was into this motley setting that the three companions made their entrance. They were not merely passers-by. They were there to stay. They were seeking their future, waiting for it to define itself more clearly. They had not come to ask for anything; they came to offer themselves.

SLEEPING ROUGH

Ignatius's premonition of 'closed windows' did not materialise. Although selfishness was rampant, there were also good people in the city of Rome. No sooner had the three pilgrim priests arrived than a generous man placed a small house at their disposal. Many years later, a son of this benefactor would remember that, when he was a small child, his father would sometimes take food to the pilgrims, who in turn shared it with people who were even worse off than they, and he also remembered that the pilgrims used to sleep on the ground. Very shortly after their arrival, the three men most probably put into effect the reason why they had come to Rome. That is to say, they placed themselves at the disposal of the pope and offered him the unconditional use of their services. In this world, where everyone came to Rome to solicit favours and to make requests, it must have been strange to see a handful of Parisian masters offering themselves for work without asking for any reward.

Soon Paul III sent Laínez and Favre to teach at the University of Rome, founded in 1303. It had been closed after the pillage of Rome in 1527 but reopened when Paul III became pope. Favre began giving lectures in theology, and Laínez attempted to do likewise, but it took some time for him to get used to the art of classroom teaching, and he tells us that even Ignatius was embarrassed by his performance. He and Favre must have spent about two years at this University. This form of instruction would have fitted in well with their training as university men, although what they were doing was a far cry from the humble tasks to which they had dedicated themselves and not in keeping with the type of work envisaged by the group.

IGNATIUS'S FAVOURITE WORK

Ignatius remained free and went back to what was now his favourite activity – conversing with people – and when he found somebody ready for his Exercises, he would encourage them to make them. The first was Doctor Ortiz: all his old suspicions in regard to Ignatius in Paris had already disappeared and he became Ignatius's enthusiastic disciple and loyal supporter. He spent forty days in Monte Cassino under his direction, making the Exercises. He claimed that Loyola had taught him a new theology, not one that a person learns in order to teach, but one that a person learns in order to live. Many others made the Exercises with the same success. These included a distinguished ambassador of the Republic of Siena, a cardinal's nephew, a medical doctor, and Cardinal Contarini, whose support would soon be of capital importance for the companions. Meanwhile, one of the companions, Hoces, died in Padua. Such, then, were the first beginnings of the three companions in Rome. Their lives bore very little likeness indeed to what they had dreamed they would be doing in Jerusalem. After Lent of 1539, they were joined by the rest of the group. All of these had gone through a very rich pastoral experience in different Italian cities, and had left behind them the living memory of numerous friendships that would later prove to be of great service.

It must have been strange beyond words to see a handful of Parisian masters offering themselves for work without asking for any reward.

Recall times in your life when you acted with generosity and self-sacrifice.

48. The Poor Pilgrim Priests, Rome 1539

PASTORAL WORK

Since there was no spare room where Ignatius and his two companions were lodged, the rest of the group had to find accommodations for themselves in the central part of Rome. They were given permission to hear confessions, to preach and to administer the sacraments. In no time at all, they were busy performing the same tasks in the city of Rome that they had done in the cities to the north. Soon, people began referring to them as 'the poor pilgrim priests'. These words very well described their appearance, their lifestyle and even their interior motivation. They would also be called 'the reformed priests', for they stood for something new and different from the ignorance, laziness and corrupt morals of many other priests.

'We began preaching in different churches,' Laínez reported. They preached on occasion also in the public squares. What surprised people most of all was that after giving their sermons, these priests went begging through the streets. Dame Poverty continued to be their chosen life-companion. Ignatius preached in Castilian in a Spanish church, and we know that several doctors of sacred theology went assiduously to hear him. One commented that never before had he seen such strength of conviction in a preacher. Ignatius was not gifted in the art of rhetoric, but he did possess the magic of the plain spoken word. All of this preaching through both word and way of life produced remarkable results. Ignatius, overwhelmed with joy, would tell his Barcelona friend, Isabel Roser, about the results of his activities, stressing that the harvest was due not to 'the talent and elegance of the presentation', but rather to the grace of God. Laínez confessed that when they spoke, there was no eloquence or style in their delivery, but a generous portion of mortification on their part. Perhaps it was precisely because of this that the power of the pure, unadorned word coming straight from the heart was more effective.

BETRAYED

Everything they did seemed to be touched by success, when suddenly the storm that Ignatius had foreseen at La Storta hit them with all its fury. He described it as 'the strongest attack and persecution' that he ever had to face. It consisted of an alarming campaign of slander and calumny that slurred the honesty and orthodoxy, not only of Ignatius, but also of the whole group. The attack was caused by the one-time serving-man of Francis Xavier, named Landívar, whose bizarre, on-again, off-again attachment to the companions had changed into enmity and fierce resentment. Having joined the companions several years earlier, he knew many things about the men who, he wrongly believed, had spurned him, and his lust for revenge encouraged him to dress up what he knew according to his taste. Ignatius, he reported, was a fugitive who had been condemned in Spain and France and had started a new religious order that was opposed to the mind of the Holy See. Was Ignatius not perhaps a Lutheran in disguise?

These accusations of heresy had the immediate effect of distancing good people from the companions. Children no longer appeared at the sermons. The dean of the College of Cardinals declared publicly that Ignatius and his followers were nothing more than wolves in sheep's clothing; some supporters discreetly distanced themselves from the companions. Soon they were held in total disrepute and saw their hopes for the apostolate dashed to the ground. What could be done to remedy the situation? As he had done on similar occasions in the past, Ignatius showed his mettle and strength of purpose, his toughness and dauntless persistence. He went to meet with Paul III and, in a most direct manner, laid bare the intention shared by his group; he told the pope in great detail about the different court trials he had undergone in Alcalá, Salamanca, Paris and Venice, and also about the sentences he had served in different prisons. Ignatius asked the pope to name a judge, anyone he wanted, and, if the companions were guilty, they would accept the proper punishment and correction, but otherwise they were to be given a formal, written declaration of their innocence.

EXONERATED

This unusual plea, so sincere and forceful, convinced the pope, who complied with Ignatius's request and ordered that a court be set up immediately. By a happy coincidence, there were men in Rome at the time who had examined Ignatius's case in Alcalá, Paris and Venice. The transactions of this case have been recently discovered and published. A clear decision was given, declaring the accused innocent. The four accusers, who had taken their cue from Landívar and were members of the Curia, were themselves later charged with heresy. One of them was sentenced to life imprisonment in Rome and, after being reconciled with the Church, died in 1559 assisted by a Jesuit father. Thus Ignatius, and this time the whole group with him, came out of the trial completely exonerated. This was the eighth examination of his orthodoxy. Ignatius had a number of copies made of the authentic transcripts of the decision and he sent them to various persons. He explained why in a covering

Ignatius was not gifted in the art of rhetoric, but he did possess the magic of the plain spoken word.

letter: 'We shall never be disturbed if we are called ignorant, rude, unskilled in speaking, or even if we are called wicked, liars and unstable men. But we were grieved that our teaching was considered unsound in this affair and that the way we have been following was thought bad. Neither the one nor the other is from ourselves: they belong to Christ and his Church.'

Ignatius celebrated his first Mass on Christmas night at Saint Mary Major's, beside a reliquary that, according to pious tradition, was the very manger in which the child Jesus had lain in Bethlehem. He had waited more than a whole year for this event, and now in this place that was a symbolic substitution for the Holy Land, he renounced his dream of going to Jerusalem.

Recall times when your speaking about the things of God had a good effect on others.

49. Finding Christ in Rome, 1539

AS THE POPE WISHES

Shortly after the whole tide of calumnies had been washed away, the companions placed themselves officially at the disposal of the pope, who by this time knew them and their mode of life. This step opened to them a horizon as broad as the Church itself, and the generosity of their intention was no less wide. But at the same time, it placed a restriction on their personal initiatives and bound their will to the pope's will. On behalf of the companions, Favre wrote to an advisor of the King of Portugal who had proposed that they be sent to preach the Gospel in the Portuguese East Indies. The justification for their refusal gives us an excellent insight into the group's spirit: 'All of us who have bound ourselves together in this Society have offered ourselves to the supreme pontiff, since he is the lord of Christ's whole harvest. When we made this offering of ourselves to him, we told him we were ready for anything that he might decide in Christ for us to do. So, should *he* send us where you propose, we will go there joyfully. Our reason for placing ourselves in this way under his will and judgement is that we know that he has a better understanding of what is best for the whole Church.' It is clear that the sense of the ecclesial was becoming more and more central in Ignatius's thinking.

A Spanish bishop had made them a similar request to that of the King of Portugal. He wanted them to go to the Americas. But they saw that the pope's will was that they should stay where they were 'because the harvest is abundant in Rome'. 'The distance of those far-off lands does not frighten us,' continued the letter, 'nor does the work involved in learning a language, provided only that this is pleasing to Christ.' The letter concludes: 'Even in Rome there are many for whom the light and truth of the Church are hateful: errors of doctrine come from errors in the way priests live, and unless these are corrected, the errors of faith will not go away.'

READY FOR ANYTHING

The ecclesial sense that is characteristic of the Society of Jesus is not the result of carefully constructed blueprints but of a will to serve. It does not mean aligning oneself with the power base of the Church, but it does mean accepting direction from the head of the Church. Paul III, who would periodically invite Favre and Laínez to his dinner table, asked them one day, 'Why do you have such a great desire to go to Jerusalem?' Then he continued, 'Italy is a true and excellent Jerusalem if you wish to reap a harvest in God's Church.' Yes indeed, the whole world was the land of Jesus, and every corner of it was in need of his word and his redemption. It was God who was now showing the crucial turning point in the road mapped out by Ignatius. Ignatius had formed his pilgrim group to be 'ready for everything', to fear no distances or strange languages, and, especially, he had given them an eagerness to integrate the message they preached with the life they lived. Their desire to serve, however, had come about from an interior motivation rather than as a response to the great religious disaster that was taking place in Europe at that time.

CONSTRUCTIVE WORK

Some like to see Ignatius's work as a bulwark against the onslaught of Lutheranism, or again they see the programme of the Jesuits as the quintessence of the Counter-Reformation. Oddly enough, the name Luther appears only once in all the writings of Ignatius. The terrible religious schism that was going on in Europe during Ignatius's lifetime does not seem to have found any literary echo in what he was determined to do, nor do we find that the resolutions made by the group of his friends were affected in any way by the religious crisis. In the Spiritual Exercises, the words 'against' and 'opposing' appear frequently, but always in the context of the conflict that takes place deep in the human heart, in the half-hearted response to the call of Christ, in the lack of freedom and generosity. Ignatius does not fight against anyone, but against that which is worst in ourselves. Goethe's words are especially pertinent in this context: 'If we take people such as they are, we make them worse than they are, but if we treat them as they should be, we will take them to where they must be taken.' Ignatius's own personal experience, and the experience he gained from dealing with different personalities and temperaments, underlines the truth of this principle. He was an excellent and convincing guide because, before guiding others, he let himself be completely guided.

Ignatius's companions were 'ready for everything'; they were available for all. Two of them were lecturing at the University of Rome, while the others were teaching children the rudiments of Christian doctrine in different quarters of the city. They now lived together in a new house that belonged to a benefactor from one of the oldest and most distinguished families in Rome. Each of them worked on his own, but they were united spiritually to face the future as a group.

The companions' horizon was as broad as the Church itself, and the generosity of their intention was no less wide.

How have your horizons grown over the years?

50. The Deliberation of the First Fathers, 1539

SERVING THE POOR

The winter of 1538 was dreadful, following a poor harvest. Food was in short supply and prices were rising. In Rome and the neighbouring area, there were months of snow storms and endless rain, and it was intolerably cold. People from nearby villages poured into the city, increasing the number of homeless crowding the streets, where some would die of hunger and exposure. Under those circumstances, for Ignatius's companions, preaching in poverty meant going out, rounding up street people and bringing them back to spend the night in their own homes. These brilliant and generous men begged for food in the streets and returned home carrying bread and wood on their shoulders, and they also brought straw, with which they made beds for the sick. They washed the beggars' feet, nursed the sick and tried to fill the stomachs of all with soup. Only then did they attempt to instruct them in the rudiments of Christian doctrine and impress upon them the need for fraternal love. Their efforts with the poor had an effect on a number of rich people and a few cardinals, who began giving alms to them. In time, the companions had to find places in Roman hospitals for the sick and starving because there were too many for them to shelter themselves. Margaret of Austria, the newly married wife of the grandson of Pope Paul III, was particularly generous in giving money to Ignatius, who scrupulously handled everything that he received without allowing any money to benefit himself or his companions, who continued to live on alms alone. Requests for their services began to come from all sides. But Ignatius waited for the missions that it would please the pope to give them. Soon the critical question arose: should they form themselves into a community with a head, to whom they would give obedience, in order to carry out better the commitment they had made to the pope?

HOW BEST TO SERVE?

Ignatius was an expert when it came to the deliberation process, and his companions were familiar with his techniques and methods. They had already chosen their permanent state of life, but its exact contours had yet to be delineated. The norms set out in the Spiritual Exercises for making a decision are found in the *Rules for the Discernment of Spirits*. These rules are valid instruments for seeking the best choice among different options. They acknowledge the different spiritual movements taking place within the individual, which is another way of stating that they help a person to become sensitive to what God is saying to the soul. The group had previously broached the problem of their future together, but without reaching perfect agreement among themselves. Now they would have to move from opinions to decisions, from speculation to a definitive, unanimous choice. The method they followed was in total accord with that prescribed elsewhere by Ignatius, that is, to pray even more fervently over the issue, to mobilise all human efforts, and then to wait on God. The human activity consisted in holding months of meetings, where the pros and cons of the question were debated and the options were examined from both a realistic and an idealistic point of view.

UNITED IN OBEDIENCE

A document titled *The Deliberation of the First Fathers* gives us a detailed account of the meetings held to determine the future of the group. Since the pope was about to deploy them in different ministries and in different places, the question was whether they should remain united as one body. They came to a unanimous decision: each one felt deep within himself that God had brought them together and united them with one another and with Ignatius who 'had engendered them in Christ', as Favre expressed it. It was clear to them that they should not dissolve this union. Not the least impressive feature of their union was the fact that they were from different national backgrounds, which historically were antagonistic toward one another. Moreover, they considered that unity as a group would endow them with greater strength and endurance when carrying out the difficult tasks to which they would be assigned.

A consequent question then arose: should they give stability and structure to the group by giving it a head to whom they would vow obedience? If they chose to do so, they would in fact be founding a new religious order. Discussion on this issue went on for many days, during which they carried on their ordinary activities and met in the evening for their deliberations. Each one reflected on his own, without discussing the question with the others and without compromising the freedom of choice of the others. They prayed all the more intensely during these days of deliberation. There was no room for giving advice or personal reflections or showing off any kind of debating abilities; rather, each one in that small group of friends told what he believed was God's will on the matter in hand. They trusted that the outcome of their deliberations would bear the characteristic stamp of the Holy Spirit: peace, interior joy and light. Ignatius throughout was not a leader imposing his will, but himself a member of the group.

'Should they form themselves into a community with a head, in order to carry out their commitment?'

THE COMPANY OF JESUS

Each of the members presented the *disadvantages* of obedience; each had to muster all the arguments and grounds against taking such a vow. On another day, they would try to evaluate the *advantages* that would accrue from taking a vow of obedience. After many days of weighing the pros and cons, they came to the unanimous decision that it was better and more expedient to give obedience to *one member* in the group in order to realise better and more accurately the original desires of the group, which consisted in doing God's will. This action would keep the group intact, enabling it to carry out the spiritual and temporal works assigned to it. On 15 April 1539, each of them signed his name to the document that had been drawn up. They numbered eleven: the six of the original Paris group – Bobadilla, Favre, Laínez, Rodrigues, Salmerón, Xavier, and then those whom Favre had admitted – Codure, Broët, Jay – with the Spaniard de Caceres, and Ignatius himself. The document in which they committed themselves to enter the Society, should the pope approve, was signed after a Mass celebrated that day by Favre, in which all of them participated.

Recall decisions you made prayerfully that brought you peace, interior joy and light.

51. 'The finger of God is here!' 1539

AVAILABILITY

Shortly after the companions had decided to form a religious congregation, the pope had Broët and Rodrigues assigned both to the reformation of monasteries of religious women in Siena and to the care of the university students there. The eleven founding fathers would never again be together as a group. Seven of those who were still in Rome on 4 May signed a further document, in which the cornerstones of the Society were laid: the members would make a special vow of obedience to the pope; each one would teach Christian doctrine to children for at least forty days each year; they would be assigned their work and their place of work by a superior; there would be a three-month period of probation for new candidates, during which time they would make the Spiritual Exercises, go on a pilgrimage, and help in hospitals. They later agreed that the task of teaching catechism to children should be included in the vows. Never during the course of history has a more democratic method been tried by the rank-and-file members of a religious order. In June, they agreed that there would be one superior general for the whole body of the Society, elected for life – something unheard of in the tradition of Canon Law. They could accept houses, but only as places to live, and also churches, but no fixed revenues could be attached to them.

The characteristic mark of the Society was availability, an availability that was particularly at the service of others and was spiritual; moreover, it was an availability that was clearly functional. There was only one contingency; *if the pope would accept it*. Ignatius, with characteristic tenacity of purpose, began to construct concrete plans for the implementation of their deliberations, while the others went off to different apostolates and accepted invitations to take on various missions. What they said and how they lived was attractive to the point of being contagious, with the result that many joined the Society.

THE FINGER OF GOD

Ignatius, that inveterate walker, remained sequestered in Rome, a prisoner of his own work. During the rest of his life, he left the city only on rare occasions. He concentrated on the future and refused to let himself be trapped by the nostalgia of his previous wanderings. It was up to him to carry out the decisions that the companions had made. He summed up the ends, means and structure of the new congregation and used the good services of his former retreatant, Cardinal Contarini, to bring the project to the attention of Pope Paul III. This was done toward the end of June 1539. The draft constituted what is a kind of Magna Carta of the Society. Pope Paul III was pleased and touched as he listened to it being read to him, and afterward he was heard to say: 'The finger of God is here!' Thus the pope's verbal approval of the Society took place on 3 September 1539. The approval by the papal Curia of the *Formula of the Institute*, as it came to be called, was all that was needed for official approbation, and such approval was considered no more than a formality.

OBSTACLES OVERCOME

What seemed to be a mere formality, however, took a whole year to untangle. A highly esteemed cardinal had difficulties with a number of points: he felt that doing away with the church organ, with the chanting of the divine office in choir, and with obligatory penances, would give Lutherans some pretext to conclude that their criticism of these Church practices was in fact justified. He also believed that the special vow to the pope was superfluous. Another opponent argued that, given the medley of so many religious orders in the Church – all of which were in need of reform and frequently quarrelled among themselves – no new religious orders should be approved. Moreover, he felt that all of the existing orders should be amalgamated into four basic groups: Dominicans, Franciscans, Cistercians and Benedictines.

Faced with this challenge, Ignatius seemed to grow in stature, implementing a maxim he would later make famous; he put all his hope in God and at the same time began to mobilise all the human resources at his disposal. As far as God was concerned, Ignatius promised that he and others would offer three thousand Masses in honour of the Blessed Trinity to obtain the sought-after grace, and as far as human resources were concerned, he turned to all the political influence he could muster. Among those who supported him were the grandson of Pope Alexander VI and the daughter of Pope Paul III. A compromise was reached by which it was agreed that the Society would be approved, but the number of professed members would be limited to sixty; however, at a later date, all restrictions could be lifted if judged expedient. At last, on 27 September 1540, Paul III signed the bull approving the Society. Known later as the *Formula of the Institute*, it was a very rich document indeed. The pope gave complete liberty to the members of the Society to name their own superior general and to draw up Constitutions especially adapted to the aims and goals of the Society.

A PATHWAY TO GOD

The bull clearly defined the purpose of the Society by employing the very terms that Ignatius had used, with the result that it sounded more like an invitation, a request, than a mere abstract definition: 'Whoever desires to serve as a soldier of God beneath the banner of the Cross in our Society, which we desire to be designated by the name of Jesus, should, after a solemn vow of chastity, keep what follows in mind. He is a member of a community founded chiefly for this purpose: to strive especially for the progress of souls in Christian life and doctrine and for the propagation of the faith by public preaching and the ministry of the Word, by Spiritual Exercises and by works of charity, and expressly by the education of children and unlettered persons in Christianity. Still further, let any such person take care to keep always before his eyes first God, and then the nature of this Institute which is, so to speak, a *pathway* to God....' The plan of life in the *Formula* was presented by the companions to the pope and 'to those who will later follow us if, God willing, we shall ever have imitators along this path'. During the course of the centuries, there would be thousands upon thousands of Jesuits who would commit themselves by now to go to any part of the world, and to live in poverty.

Pope Paul III was pleased and touched as he listened, and was heard to say: 'The finger of God is here!'

How do you experience the invitation 'to keep God always before your eyes'?

52. Ignatius Elected General, 1541

XAVIER TO THE EAST

In September 1540, when the Society was formally approved, there was barely a dozen committed companions and they were already so spread out that their members could not come together to celebrate the pontifical approbation of their Society. They considered that service to others was paramount and that celebrating the birth of their Society was of secondary importance. The Portuguese ambassador wanted ten Jesuits to be sent to the far-off Indies. 'Señor Ambassador,' Ignatius replied, 'what will Your Lordship leave for the rest of the world?' Nevertheless, he designated two for the Indies: Rodrigues, who at the time was in Siena, and Bobadilla, who was in Naples. Although suffering from fever, the former boarded a ship bound for Lisbon on 5 March 1540; the latter travelled by foot to Rome with the intention of catching a ship there. But when he arrived, he was in such a wretched state that the house physician declared his making a trip to Portugal unthinkable. Ignatius was also sick at the time, but was under pressure to find a last-minute substitute for Bobadilla. He had one candidate in Rome: Xavier. He summoned Xavier and entrusted the mission to him. 'Master Francis, you already know that at the bidding of His Holiness two of our group must go to India, and that Master Bobadilla was chosen as one of these. He cannot travel because of his illness, and the ambassador cannot wait until he is well. This is a task for you!' 'Good enough! I am ready,' was Xavier's reply.

Master Xavier hastily sewed up the tattered parts of an old pair of pants and his cassock and went off to receive the pope's blessing. He then bade farewell to his companions, leaving with them the written formula of his vows, his vote for the coming election for a general, and his approval of all the constitutions, rules and ordinances that his companions who remained behind would draw up. The following day, he rode out with the ambassador toward Lisbon. There he would have to wait another nine months for the ship destined for the Indies. Finally, on 7 April 1541, he set sail for Goa. The sick Rodrigues remained in Portugal, but an Italian Jesuit embarked with Xavier. The crossing was very difficult; the ship was obliged to spend the winter in Mozambique and did not arrive in Goa until the spring of 1542. Thus it was that Xavier began the adventure that would make him the indisputable giant of missionary activity. His was not a matter of aspiring for any particular mission, but rather it was a firm lived-out mindset expressed in the formula 'ready for everything'. So it was that on the day of the confirmation of the Society, there were only three of the original members in the Eternal City.

RELUCTANT GENERAL

On 4 March 1541, Ignatius and five companions came together in Rome. It was agreed that the task of drafting Constitutions should be handed over to Ignatius and Codure, and that the success of the operations of the Society needed a strong and steady hand at the helm. Therefore, it was necessary to determine who would be the head. 'Up until this time,' Polanco would later write, 'Ignatius had steered the rudder of their little boat more like a father who had begotten them all in the Spirit, or as a friend who had gained their complete confidence by his prudence and charity, than like a superior who had been invested with legitimate powers to govern them.' In April 1541, as expected, Ignatius was elected unanimously by the ten other companions. Those who voted gave reasons for their choice. Xavier expressed himself in these moving terms: 'Ignatius is the one who brought us together with no little effort and who will also, not without effort, be able to preserve, rule, and make us advance from good to better, since he knows us best.'

The other five who were present in Rome when the ballots were counted were overjoyed, but not Ignatius. He tells us in some jottings 'how he felt in his soul' in regard to the acceptance of the election results. He stated that he would prefer to be governed than to govern; that he did not feel capable of directing himself, much less anyone else. He spoke of his many bad habits, past and present, and of his many sins, his faults and his miseries. He begged his companions to reflect for three days on the subject, 'in order to find someone who could fulfil this office better for all concerned'. They agreed to this proposal, 'although not very willingly'. At the end of four days, the vote was taken again and the results were the same as before. Ignatius decided that he would leave the decision in the hands of his confessor, and he went off to the Franciscan convent, where for three days he made his confession of all his sins, 'since the day he was able to sin, down to the present time', and also all his infirmities and bodily miseries.

On Easter Sunday, his confessor let him know in unmistakable terms his decision, that Ignatius should accept the result: not to do so was tantamount to resisting the Holy Spirit. Ignatius asked his confessor to reflect more in the Lord over what he had said and to come to a peaceful solution. After this, the confessor should write out his decision on a piece of paper, enclose it in a sealed envelope addressed to the Society, and send it to his companions. Three days later, the confessor sent his reply, stating that 'Ignatius should take in hand the affairs and direction of the Society'. So he had to accept and

'Master Francis, this is a task for you!' 'Good enough! I am ready,' was Xavier's reply.

resign himself to the task. A few days later, having visited the traditional seven churches of Rome, the group came together in the Basilica of Saint Paul outside-the-walls, where they confessed to one another. Then they made their profession and, when Mass was over, they embraced one another in a brotherly fashion. 'Thus they concluded their profession and the vocation they were beginning' and returned to where they lived.

How ready have you found yourself over the years to do God's will?

53. Prisoner in Rome, 1540-56

UNCERTAINTY GONE

All of Ignatius's uncertainties about the future were now past; the way forward had been marked and sanctioned by the papal approval of the Society of Jesus in September 1540. Ignatius had dreamed of Jerusalem but awakened in Rome. He had come to the city without thinking of founding a religious order, but now he found himself a superior general. He had loved anonymity, radical poverty, naked hope in God alone, pilgrim routes, and hospices, and from now on he would be visited and solicited by ambassadors, bishops, hangers-on and favourites of popes and cardinals, and all the while he would be condemned to an immobile, sedentary life, a prisoner of his own work. He had desperately wanted to live and die in some obscure corner of Palestine, but now he found himself at the very centre of Christendom, where he could feel the weary heartbeat of the Church and also realise his own impotence in the face of so many needs. Everything had changed. Without his even realising it, God had taken him to this new scene. All that remained unchanging was his firm commitment to work for the greater glory of God, for the help of souls, and to be of service however he could.

The pathway was set within the context and structure of the hierarchical Church. From this moment on, the Society and Ignatius would be as inseparable from one and other as the Pietà and the Sistine Chapel are from Michelangelo. Ignatius was now the Society and the Society was Ignatius, and both were inserted into the Church. It would be through the Society that he would make a gift of his life to the Church, a gift given hour after hour, day after day, down to his last moment on the day of his death. There were still fifteen years left for him to live, and this he did in a state of poor health, which brought him, on a number of occasions, close to death's door.

CONTEMPLATIVE STANCE

It is not easy for a biographer to separate the story of Ignatius from that of his work, to isolate his life-story from the account of the expansion of the Society during his lifetime. The problem is dealing with these parallel histories without getting lost in an ocean of details. Decidedly, we must limit ourselves to Ignatius, the helmsman of the Society, the blacksmith who forged the institution and its men, the patient, reflective Ignatius, who was ever open to the vast world and the needs of the time, and who was especially disposed to hearing the silent voice of the Spirit. His external aspect radiated a quality that defined his personality: he was a contemplative in the broadest sense of that term, someone who was always thinking in a reflective way. Even though he lived in the company of others, he had a solitary dimension: he would pace up and down in his own room or in the garden, stopping now and then to raise his eyes heavenward, thinking, always thinking. From this moment on, the high adventure in his life was a thing of the past; in terms of pure narrative, there is not much more to say. His life became more concentrated as the deepest part of his personality hid itself. In order to penetrate that mystery, we must look at what he did, what he wrote and what he planned for the future.

ADMINISTRATION FOR THE WORLD

Ignatius had wanted to help and to serve, but it was now his lot to direct, co-ordinate and order. But he believed that humility and charity should distinguish the one who is put in charge. For this reason, he immediately placed himself at the disposal of the house cook so that he could be put to work doing the most humble tasks. But he was serious and scrupulous in his performance of his kitchen chores, giving himself to them with novice-like fervour. Later, he had to divide the time he spent in the kitchen with his growing administrative duties, and, finally, he would have to give up the kitchen altogether. He took pleasure in handing his kitchen job over to his brother Jesuits, some of them brilliant academicians, who took up where he had left off.

Close to where Ignatius lived was the Church of Santa Maria della Strada, which was made over to him in 1541, when its owner joined the Society. Later, he managed to acquire the garden adjacent to the church, and there in 1544 he built a residence for some thirty Jesuits. In 1602, a new and larger building was erected to take the place of the 1544 residence. The four tiny rooms in the older building, where Ignatius lived, worked and died, were saved and may be visited today. These rooms also served as the working and living space for the next two superior generals, Laínez and Saint Francis Borgia. In Ignatius's time, they had already become the heart of the Society because into them poured news from every corner of the world and out of them were sent countless administrative directives. In these rooms, for twelve years, Ignatius prayed, reflected and made decisions.

The name of the Church of Santa Maria della Strada – Saint Mary of the Way – suited men who spent their lives travelling and who were ever ready to take on the challenge of new horizons. Who could ever tell the miles travelled on land and sea by the greatest of these travellers, Francis Xavier? Who could add up all the distances covered by the other companions who had been sent to Ireland, Ethiopia and Brazil, and who could map out all of the roads walked upon by that indefatigable traveller, Pierre Favre, who crisscrossed Italy, Germany, France, Spain and Portugal before he died, exhausted, on his way to attend the Council of Trent?

Ignatius had dreamed of Jerusalem but awakened in Rome.

To the ends of the earth

Recall some of the unexpected turns that your life has taken. Can you see God's hand in them?

54. Caring for the Poor

TALKING TO CHILDREN

Ignatius took on many personal apostolic activities, especially during his early years in Rome. During the summer of 1541, he deliberately set aside forty days to teach catechism to children, a task he also required of his brethren through the Constitutions. Was he attracted to this apostolate because it seemed so insignificant and modest, especially when it was done by masters from the University? It was a practical, no-nonsense way to put into practice his old desire 'to preach in poverty'. His language must have been frightful, a sorry mishmash of Latin, Italian and Spanish, because the very young Ribadeneira, who had just then entered the Society, confessed that he had to blush whenever he heard Ignatius speaking. With more courage than the others, this young man confronted Ignatius and told him about the mistakes he was making. As a result, Ignatius asked him to correct him whenever he erred, but in a very short time Ribadeneira gave up trying because Ignatius's grammatical mistakes were so many and so shocking. We have already stressed that neither oratory nor elegance of style was Ignatius's strong suit, but no one would question the strength and the weight that he gave to the words he spoke and wrote. The people who heard him realised how deeply he believed what he preached.

He would never again repeat in any extended way this catechetical experience. However, during the years that followed, he would sometimes stop in streets or public squares to address a few words to the children. In 1606 during his beatification process, there were still people living in Rome who recalled the little sermons he would sometimes give while standing next to the della Strada church or elsewhere. One witness stated how he learned the Our Father and Hail Mary from the lips of Ignatius. Another reported an unexpected anecdote: 'I remember Father Ignatius preaching. The boys were throwing apples at him, but he went on patiently giving his sermon, without becoming angry.' These events took place in 1552, four years before he died.

PROSTITUTION

Circumstances determined how the goal of 'helping souls' was to be translated into projects. Ignatius confronted problems endemic to the big city, not those that affected the high and mighty, but rather those that were particular to the seamy side of the city. He showed exceptional gifts for organising programmes and in setting up networks that proved to be effective long after he was involved. He would identify the problem, make the community aware of it, involve others in finding a solution, set up an institution to implement an agreed plan of action, and finally he would put the whole project under the patronage of the pope.

The first open wound he attempted to heal was the very old profession of prostitution. Rome was a paradise for prostitutes who flocked there from every corner of Europe. It was not easy rescuing these women and it was even more difficult to find any of them who wanted to be rescued. Ignatius spoke of his project with a number of influential people, but they did not move from giving advice to action. Then, by good fortune, a number of marble pieces dating from the time of Pompey were unearthed when the foundations of the new Jesuit residence were being prepared. Ignatius sold these pieces and, although the money was desperately needed to augment the house's meagre budget, he summoned up the courage he reserved for grand occasions and credited the money to this project that was so dear to his heart, with these words: 'Since no one else wants to be first, then follow me; I'll be first.' The action was bold and it marked the beginning of a house of refuge that would continue in existence for centuries. Ignatius wrote constitutions for the house and founded a confraternity that would care for it, and he received a commitment from fourteen cardinals and ladies recruited from the highest echelons of the nobility who would serve as trustees. He then had the pope write a bull giving official approbation to his project. A woman was appointed director of the house, while the spiritual progress of the inmates was the responsibility of Ignatius for a number of years. By 1552, some three hundred women had passed through this establishment.

It was not an exceptional sight to see Ignatius walking the streets of Rome followed at a discreet distance by a woman whom he had persuaded to take refuge at the house, named Santa Marta. For all their sardonic wit, the Roman populace gave respectful silence to Ignatius's activities, although there were some disappointed lovers, such as the head postmaster of the pontifical mail, who resorted to violence when his beloved turned herself in to Santa Marta. He came at night to throw stones at the house and to scream obscene accusations against Ignatius and his companions. Ignatius stood his ground, but, as he had done on many other occasions, he went to the pope and asked for a formal investigation that would clarify matters. This was to safeguard the public reputation of the Society. The judgement was made public, but afterward Ignatius interceded so that his accuser would not be punished.

'Since no one else wants to be first, then follow me; I'll be first.'

TO HELP EVEN ONE

Ignatius has gone down in history as a man who was able to get things done, and what he did here in this slimy underworld was unique, although the methods he used were characteristic of how he operated in other areas as well. When someone pointed out that many of these women would soon return to their evil ways, he responded that if, out of love of Christ, just one of these women gave up sinning for a single night, all his efforts would be rewarded. No amount of fatigue, he said, could induce him to give up in his efforts to rescue one single sinner, even though he knew that she might soon return to her former life. This is vintage Ignatius – the same reply that he gave to his brother in 1535, who had predicted that his catechetical efforts in his home town of Azpeitia would come to naught.

When social problems confront you, do you ever see your way to helping even a single person involved?

55. Early Years of the Society

CARING FOR THOSE AT RISK

Ignatius knew that it would be better to prevent the illness of prostitution than to try to cure it, so he supported a recently founded group called 'The Society of Wretched Young Women'. He did no little work for this group by rescuing girls of ten and twelve from an environment that would inevitably lead them into prostitution. Another field to which he turned his personal attention was the issue of the Jews. The Spanish obsession regarding purity of blood, a consequence of the expulsion of the Jews from Spain, permeated not only civil society but also ecclesiastical institutions. But it had no hold on Ignatius. He had no difficulty in admitting people of Jewish ancestry to the Society. On one occasion, Ignatius astonished his guests at table by saying in a most convincing way: 'I would consider it a special grace from our Lord to come from a line of Jewish ancestry because I would then be able to be a person related, according to the flesh, to Christ our Lord and our Lady, the glorious Virgin Mary.' Such a statement was a source of scandal to more than one of the guests.

Ignatius took his apostolate among the Jews very seriously. First and foremost, he sought to remove barriers that made the conversion of Jews to Christianity difficult. Converted Jews were forced to turn over all their fortune to tax collectors and they lost all their hereditary rights. Ignatius obtained a bull from Pope Paul III in 1532, abolishing such customs. He began welcoming into his own home Jews who wanted to be baptised, and he instructed them in the faith. Margaret of Austria, and later the pope, constructed hospices for Jews and all non-baptised people who wanted to become Christians. Ignatius also promoted and supported the creation of houses for orphans and street waifs. His blueprints for action suggest more an attitude open to involvement and enthusiasm rather than specific programmes that should always be implemented whatever the circumstances. Because he was concerned about human suffering not in a theoretical but in a concrete way, Ignatius responded with all his heart to real situations, to hunger and to moral decadence. He was good and compassionate toward victims of racial prejudice, a friend to children and to the poor in spirit, but a rigorous opponent of heresy, as when he supported the setting up of the Roman Inquisition in 1542.

EXPANDING NUMBERS

These apostolic activities, however, were sideline operations, complementary at most to the main task of governing the Society. This Society was expanding, and Ignatius's task included giving it a form, creating a framework for it, endowing it with Constitutions, in short, institutionalising it. Such an enterprise required that he should put shackles on his apostolic spirit. But he was no longer alone. Ignatius had at last realised his old dream of gathering around him some companions like himself. From 1540 to 1556, the date of Ignatius's death, the number of his followers passed from a dozen to almost one thousand. What was the secret of this phenomenal growth? There were other congregations with the same ideals and similar apostolic undertakings, yet none would acquire the numerical population or the historical importance of the Society. Was it because of the so-called 'modernity' of the Society's way of life, which was versatile and adaptable? Or because of its flying-squadron-like apostolates, which were geared toward action and were more disciplined and generous than those of others? Did it come from the Society's rugged, even heroic, spirit, its remarkable corporate dedication to follow Christ and to serve others in a counter-cultural manner, one that took for granted a radical rejection of the impulses that enslave people – pride, sensuality, riches, or was it because the Society chose for its field of action the whole wide world?

ATTRACTING THE YOUNG

It is clear that the Society grew by some strange kind of osmosis or contagion. Ignatius was the one who attracted and conquered many, who, having once been seduced, became themselves seducers. At the beginning, those who attached themselves to the Society were mature men, university professors, canons, pontifical chamberlains, all of whom changed their lives and their horizons. Young men, too, began knocking at the door. Some were distinguished, others from modest backgrounds. All of them found in the Ignatian way an ideal that challenged them. Many came with minds already made up; others were goaded on by various happenings in their lives. One young man, uncertain of the future, had come to Italy to seek his fortune: a meeting with Ignatius decided his future. Another, a thirteen-year-old page, Pedro Ribadeneira, was forced to run away from the Cardinal's palace where he had been lodged, because he had a penchant for fighting, and was given refuge at Santa Maria della Strada, where, in no time, he became the house mascot. Ignatius won him over for ever through the Spiritual Exercises. He later became Ignatius's first biographer: his name was Pedro Ribadeneira.

Ignatius realised that he would never have an adequate intake of mature and educated men who would be immediately available to meet his pressing needs. So he set up houses of formation for generous young men who flocked to join him. The human and spiritual fibre of those in formation had to be proven by trials. Each candidate had to go through a time of spiritual training that included making the Spiritual Exercises and a month of service in the hospitals. Then would come the experiment that for Ignatius was charged with memories, the pilgrimage 'made on foot and without money, putting all hope in the Creator and Lord and accepting to sleep poorly and eat badly, because it seems to us that the one who cannot walk for a day without eating or sleeping poorly cannot persevere long in our Society'. Neither weaklings nor impractical romantics had a place in Ignatius's ranks.

'The one who cannot walk for a day without eating or sleeping poorly cannot persevere long in our Society.'

Recall someone whose idealism attracted you to go beyond yourself.

56. Forming his Followers

SHAPING IDEALISTS

Ignatius explained in personnel management terminology the reason for his 'great experiments' in forming novices. The monk, he wrote, is protected by the religious cloister and the tranquillity and peaceful atmosphere of the monastery, but the Jesuit travels from place to place. The novice in a monastery is given a long time to correct any former bad habits and to seek perfection, whereas the Jesuit has to be proven and well-tested before he is admitted to the Society, because, in a very short time, he will be plunged into the world and, therefore, will need to have more strength and experience, and greater gifts and graces from God. Although Ignatius did not bear the title of Master of Novices, he personally oversaw the formation of new members, both the mature and the younger aspirants. He did not seek out geniuses as recruits, but honest, upright men who had been conquered by an ideal. He had the habit of delegating responsibilities, and, as a consequence, he was able to transform men of middling talents into tireless and effective workers. By so acting, he created a style that became self-perpetuating.

MILD AND FRIENDLY

Those who entered the Society in Rome came to know Ignatius. Although somewhat isolated where they were lodged, they nevertheless partook of the life of the community, and could drink in the spirit and the manner of life of the early members. Those who passed through Ignatius's hands retained an unforgettable picture of the physical and spiritual portrait of their incomparable formation director. The young Majorcan Nadal, who would have nothing to do with Ignatius in Paris, was already a priest and a doctor when he fell into Ignatius's net. He had read a long letter from Xavier, who described his own apostolic activities. As a result, he came to Rome, made the Exercises that years earlier he had refused to make, and entered the Society. In the days that followed, Ignatius assigned this brilliant doctor as helper to both the cook and the gardener. On one occasion, as Ignatius walked about the garden in the company of a theologian, Nadal, who was an acknowledged authority on Latin and Hebrew, did his best to keep his mouth closed and stick to his job of shovelling the sod. His trial lasted four months, but then he was excused from making the hospital experiment and, because of his health, he did not have to make a pilgrimage. He never forgot Ignatius's 'mildness and friendliness' in his dealings with him, or the visits Ignatius paid him in his room, or the times he invited him to eat at his table and to take a walk with him. Ignatius dispensed Nadal from fasting, and when Nadal protested that this would shock the others, Ignatius responded: 'You tell me who gets scandalised and I'll throw him out of the Society.' The image that makes Ignatius out to be inflexible is very wide of reality.

HUMOROUS

Another novice of Ignatius recalled with pathos the difficulties he had begging in the streets of Rome and having to put up with so many insults. The one that cost him the most was delivered by a former companion of his university days. This man was shocked when he saw the novice dressed in a cassock and begging, and he began to upbraid him on his lifestyle, even trying to get him to leave the Society by telling him that he was the joke of Rome. Serving in the kitchen cost this man just as much, if not more, than that particular incident. He was squeamish and had a horror of dirt and he found it very difficult to overcome his repugnance when exposed to it. On one occasion, as he emerged from a cellar covered with dust and cobwebs, he ran into Ignatius in the corridor. Ignatius smiled at him and said: 'I like you better this way.'

WINNING THE HEART

Yet another novice recalled how Ignatius used to invite him, in a most gentle way, to come and sit side by side with him for a chat in the garden or elsewhere. When this novice was ill, Ignatius came to visit him and treated him as a father would treat his son. At other times, Ignatius would call him to his table and offer him an apple or a pear that he had taken meticulous pains to peel. He recalled that Ignatius's manner of speaking was admirable, always grave, never excited, and that his words were never empty or superficial, but always powerful and efficacious. He seemed to have thought over everything he said and no one left his presence without being consoled. He seemed always turned toward God, even when many things were on his mind. He had immense trust in God and he was capable of taking bold action in moments of crisis. He also had confidence in his men: the newly appointed rector of the Roman College asked Ignatius for precise directives, but he answered: 'Fit the rules to the circumstances. Do as you see best and the Holy Spirit will illumine you.' When he enquired about which members of the community should be assigned to what jobs, Ignatius responded: 'Tailor the clothes to match the cloth you have at hand.' Ignatius was unquestionably an extraordinary judge and maker of men. His principal method was 'to gain the man's heart by a

Ignatius seemed to have thought over everything he said, and no one left his presence without being consoled.

very supportive, gentle, fatherly love'. He had a real and sincere love for each, expressed in words and deeds; he trusted everyone; he took into account each man's personality and situation and was open to the particular needs of each.

So from 1540 onward, Ignatius became a desk-bound administrator. Instead of travelling himself, he followed the steps of each member of the 'least Society', as he liked to call it. He took great pleasure in greeting his Jesuit companions who, during that generous and adventurous springtime of the early Society, arrived in Rome laden with all sorts of stories. He could not hide his joy at seeing them, and his meetings with them could lead to those rare occasions when he seemed to lose control of himself and break out in loud laughter. He said to one happy novice: 'Laugh, my son, and be joyful in the Lord, for a religious has no reason to be sad and a thousand reasons to rejoice!'

When people leave you, do they go away consoled?

180

57. 'Ready for everything'

GOD AS LEADER

Ignatius is often presented as a genius of military strategy, able to identify the flashpoints of tension throughout the world, devise a plan of action, send out the Society, diversify its ministries and, finally, launch seasoned troops on all fronts. But rather than planning events, Ignatius was in fact towed along by what was happening, confident that God was doing the steering and leading him through the events taking place around him. He was a captain; his sailing craft was shipshape, and these events were the winds billowing the sails and directing the ship's course. There were the pope's peremptory demands as well as repeated petitions on the part of bishops, cardinals, kings and princes. Ignatius did not choose countries or cities to work in; he listened to requests, and then, after he had ascertained the men he had available, he made his decisions.

During the first years of its existence, the Society was ruled by the unforeseeable. The pope decided where the members were to go among heretics and pagans, while the European theatre seemed to be more under the direction of Ignatius, who was at the mercy of those making demands on him. But there was something unmistakeable in everything that Ignatius did – action. And it was always an action that was enormously diversified and even disconcerting. He hardly had time to think about the Society itself, to allow his directives for the various ministries to take root and to enact rules. The exigencies of everyday life prevailed over everything. In this mad springtime of the Society, every year witnessed innovations that compelled him to deploy men and to take on projects, to search out new points of Canon Law, to be in a state of constant evolution, not to close doors but to enact rules that would be both adaptable and flexible.

RAPID EVOLUTION

In its first ten years, 1541–51, the Society evolved more than it would during the next four centuries. Ignatius was both a dreamer and a most pragmatic man, always adjusting to circumstances. For instance, he had intended that the early companions should preach in poverty, but later he came to require that those joining the Society should have a solid academic background. So, as mentioned earlier, he set up colleges for newly received members, but then he opened them to non-Jesuits as well, and so they multiplied in cities throughout Italy, Spain and Germany and became one of the characteristic works of the Society. Stability, a characteristic of the older monastic way of life, had no place among Ignatius's followers, for their lives were patterned on mobility and total availability. The early Jesuits were spread out far away from one another; no community life, no regular house; sent in pairs or alone, depending on some charitable person to put them up or finding lodging in hospices. Ignatius had confidence in his men once they were sufficiently matured, but especially he had confidence in God. He wanted his men to be 'ready for everything'.

CHOICES

Ignatius said Yes to missions among non-believers and to supplying theologians for the Council of Trent, to helping the hungry, instructing Jewish converts, bringing spiritual aid to soldiers, redeeming prisoners, and reforming monasteries of religious women. However, he said No to giving spiritual direction on an ordinary basis to religious women, and No to ecclesiastical offices, and, more precisely, to bishoprics. He believed that opening the door to such offices would spell the ruin of the Society and that it would be a source of confusion for generous young men who joined the Society because they wanted a more austere and difficult lifestyle. He said No to a particular religious dress; his men were to dress in the manner of ordinary, honest priests; No also to chanting the office in choir, because it limited mobility and availability for work. Likewise, he said No to solemn chant and to having an organ at liturgies, No to the scourge and to other monastic penances, and to long hours of personal prayer, which was a common practice among religious, particularly in Spain. Jesuit students should make their study a prayer and find God in their daily preoccupations and in the people with whom they met.

Ignatius thus opened up wide horizons and also marked out frontiers. Between these, he established a style of life and work, and through them he was hammering out the particular form the Society was beginning to take.

Pope Paul III, who had so willingly approved the Society, proceeded to honour it by raining down upon it a veritable torrent of protective documents. Before the Society was ten years old, it possessed privileges that the Franciscans and Dominicans had not been able to obtain for centuries. After the old days of trusting in God alone, had come the era of receiving favours, protection, privileges, and in the wake of these came all the inevitable resentments attached to them.

LIVING POVERTY

In all of this, Ignatius remained obsessed by his ideals of poverty. For him, poverty was the school in which one learnt confidence in God, a concrete way in which one could imitate Christ, and a compelling witness when teaching the Gospel to others. The days when he had had a personal spontaneous effect on others had passed; now he had to think of how to transmit to an institution the spirit of living poverty. His deliberation of pros and cons is not simply a monologue, the product of an introspective reflection, but a dialogue between himself and the transcendent, the divine. His *Spiritual Diary,* written in the spring of 1544, opens to us unexpected vistas in the soul of this Christian who knew that God is not infallibly found at the end of our efforts as a reward for what we have achieved, but rather is Someone who comes to us gratuitously and with open hands. The twenty-five pages that remain of this *Spiritual Diary* reveal Ignatius's deepest secret, namely, that he was a great mystic. They show him in dialogue with the divine as he sought for light and for confirmation of the promptings through which God speaks to us and guides us.

> *Ignatius was confident that God was doing the steering and leading him through the events taking place around him.*

At the pope's service

> Are you confident that God is leading you through the events that make up your life?

58. A Busy Mystic

THE GIFT OF TEARS

Ignatius's *Spiritual Diary* reveals to us something of the unfathomable depths of the mystical experiences, focused on the Trinity, that centred about his celebration of the Mass. The natural modesty of this taciturn and undemonstrative Basque made it more difficult for him to express what all mystics acknowledge to be indescribable. Basically, one can say that he carried his secret with him to the grave, although these precious pages give us some snatches of his secret and his personality and reveal that before all else he was a man infused with the gifts of the Holy Spirit, one who listened to God all the time.

With him, each word is rugged and endowed with a tremendous power of muted suggestion, like a piece of granite dug from a quarry. He speaks of 'abundance of devotion, internal and external tears'; 'I realised things in such a way that cannot be described'; 'I felt a deep understanding, delightful and very spiritual, full of warm devotion and very sweet'. His experiences came to him while he was saying Mass, but also while he was walking along the city streets or sitting at the dinner table or waiting in the ante-chamber of a cardinal. His mystical experiences in no way deterred him from his normal activities, nor did they induce him to seek a more isolated, retired life. Neither did these experiences take on the nuptial symbolism characteristic of so many other mystics. In his case, mysticism is translated into service, the dynamism of a truth he loves and cherishes, which is the source of endless tears. Who would have believed it! The titan of action and of immense energy was a man whose eyes were ruined by mystical tears. He alludes to this gift of tears 175 times in the pages of the *Spiritual Diary*. No painter has been able to depict those eyes that once spoke and that now, lying behind his death mask, are lifeless. In Padua, a man described him as 'that tiny little Spaniard with a bit of a limp and sparkling eyes'. Ignatius was indeed very short, which explains why, just a few years after his death, a preacher contrasted Ignatius's greatness with his unimpressive bodily appearance, referring to him as 'a tiny grain', 'so small a man' and 'the little man of God'.

FORGING HIS MEN

Although a mystic, Ignatius lived with his feet on the ground and was enmeshed in thousands of prosaic duties and dull day-to-day work, giving himself to a multiplicity of ministries, particularly to what he considered to be the most important task of all – forging his men and forming his 'least Society', which had just seen the light of day and had already become the 'dispersed Society'. He had to set guidelines for the Order and also maintain the unity and cohesion of its members, scattered as they were over the face of the earth. Ignatius had a sense for the concrete; he was not at home with either abstractions or vague ideas. Câmara, to whom he dictated his *Autobiography,* described this trait in a charming fashion: 'He never persuades with sentiments but with facts ... he never dresses up realities with words, but he presents all the circumstances and details, which are so convincing that they almost force a person to be persuaded.... His manner of speaking is simple, clear and distinct. And he has such a keen memory for past events, and even the key words associated with a particular event, that he can tell what took place ten, fifteen, and even more years ago, exactly as it happened.' For Ignatius, as for any true Basque, the word had a tremendous importance because the word conveys the person. This is why he spoke and wrote only after having spent a long time reflecting on what he wanted to say.

GOOD PSYCHOLOGY

Ignatius's instructions – there are more than two hundred of them – offer us a wonderful insight into his personality and way of acting. They reveal the breadth and variety of the Society's early ministries, their geographical spread, their success, but, most particularly, they give us examples of Ignatius's personal criteria, motives and objectives and the profound evangelical spirit that animated everything he did. Moreover, we notice in them a first-class psychologist, used to dealing with people. When in 1541 he sent Broët and Salmerón on an exceedingly ticklish mission to Ireland, he gave them some very provocative pieces of advice. They should speak little and listen long. When they communicated with people of influence, they should size each one up and adapt themselves to the temperament of the person, like Saint Paul who became all things to everyone. He suggested that they should take on the ways of those they hoped to influence: that they be well armed through self-examination, ready to put up with anything and not lose composure. They should be guarded in speech, and remember that everything a person says in private may later become public. He wanted them to be generous in giving time to everyone; if they promised to have something done for tomorrow, do it today. They should enter by the other's door and

Before all else, Ignatius was a man who listened to God all the time.

come out by their own, 'in order to net the person for the greater service of God'.

FAILURE IN IRELAND

Despite all this advice, the Irish mission of 1541 was a total disaster. In Lyons, Salmerón and Broët had met the Scottish primate, Cardinal Beaton, who was also an archbishop and the father of six children, and who, four years later, would be hacked to death in his bedroom by his own countrymen. Beaton told the two nuncios that, of all humankind, the Irish were perhaps the wildest and the most incapable of any kind of discipline whatsoever. Perhaps his arguments had some influence on them. In any case, they spent a month in Ireland, where the bishops in twenty-two of the thirty dioceses had already disavowed the pope's authority in favour of that of Henry VIII. The fact that the two nuncios from Rome were able to leave Ireland alive was regarded by some as being a near miracle. On their way back to Rome, in their dirty and tattered cassocks, they were taken for spies and were thrown into prison in Lyons. Salmerón was not exaggerating when he wrote: 'Ireland was not without its share of the cross of Christ our Lord, for we suffered hunger and thirst, and had no place to put our heads or even a place to say an Our Father in peace.'

Do you find that, as you move on in life, you listen to God more?

59. Instructions and Letters

COUNCIL OF TRENT

Ignatius's instructions to Laínez and Salmerón on their being sent to the Council of Trent are of great interest and worth. Ignatius recommended that they pray hard and have others also pray for the success of the Council. He advised them to be good listeners and to be cautious in dealing with controversial matters. They should not take their own time or comfort into consideration as long as they were at the service of the people of Trent. They were to preach, hear confessions, teach children, give the Exercises, visit hospitals, exhort the people to devotion and prayer and help them to come to a fuller knowledge of themselves and a greater love of God. By speaking 'at length, in a practical way, lovingly, and with affection', they were to encourage everyone to renew their spiritual lives. They should be solicitous in maintaining union among themselves, practise fraternal correction and revise together their daily agenda.

Ignatius had sent his men to Trent 'more out of obedience than because he thought they could be of any help, even in the smallest matter pertaining to the Council'. But a few days after their arrival on 18 May 1546, they were inscribed on the list of theologians. Very shortly, both men were in the limelight, making interventions. In the next session of the Council, 1551–52, they would be listed as pontifical theologians, which was no obstacle to the fact that they were lodged in a cramped, dingy room with only one bed and no table at which they could read or write. They again intervened in the conciliar discussions, but they did not on this account give up their preferred ministries – hearing confessions, teaching catechism and visiting hospitals. By their appearance at the Council, they made the newly formed Society known, and so, from that moment on, there was an increase in the number of bishops from Italy, France and Spain who would open their dioceses to Jesuits.

LITTLE TIME TO EAT

What was conspicuous about these former masters of the University of Paris was not only their theological learning but the quality of their lives and their apostolic zeal. The secret of their impact lay in their priesthood. They were authentic, effective priests. They performed the so-called customary ministries, that is, either a permanent ministry carried out from a single residence or house by two companions, or a temporary stay of two companions in a given city. The only novelty was that the companions were conscientious in performing their pastoral duties, duties that, unfortunately, the local clergy had neglected. Ignatius and his followers insisted on going into the very heart of people and their culture. They encouraged those who were well-disposed, but they did not forget the abandoned masses. They were able to pass a whole day hearing confessions and taking barely enough time to eat. The seeds they sowed fell on multitudes of people, on monasteries that were beginning to reform and on individuals who wanted a deeper spiritual life. Their efforts changed the lives of many priests and canons; they attracted generous young men to the Society and they encouraged the laity to become involved in activities that they had never previously considered. Furthermore, they tried to ensure that what they began would continue after they left. In this service, we cannot discern what was planned and what was an improvised response to immediate and fundamental needs. Whatever the case, they poured themselves out unsparingly, down to complete physical exhaustion. Spread out as they were from home base and from one another, the lives of these first Jesuits were exposed to all types of adversities and marked by personal responsibility.

KEEPING IN TOUCH

Initially the Society had been an adventure of closely bonded friends. Simplicity was the keynote in their dealings with one another. In Rome, for example, Francis Xavier once surprised a visitor by simply calling out: 'Hey, Ignatius, Araoz is here!' As numbers grew, such ease and deep friendship was impossible to sustain among men who met one another only fleetingly. Only the slow mail of the sixteenth century could keep affective bonds alive, allow for exchanges of news, and ensure that the same manner of living was adhered to by all. Ignatius insisted with his followers that writing letters was not a pastime but an obligation. He led by example: we have some seven thousand of his letters, but he wrote many more. In one, he recounts that he had sent 250 letters out in one night. He took great pains over them, chiselled words and sentences, corrected and redrafted them. His norm to his brethren was: 'What one writes must be considered more carefully than what one says, because the written word remains and is a witness for all times.'

Ignatius's letters show his mind and personality: in them he reveals his top priorities, his worries, his mettle before adversity and in face of confrontation, his flexibility, affection, gratitude and patience. He narrates, counsels, exhorts and gives orders. He sets out plans for unbelievable undertakings, such as a crusade against the Turks. He addresses every single correspondent pleasantly and with grave courtesy, and gives a word of parting that comes from affection and points toward transcendence: 'May it please God that we may know his most holy will and fulfil it perfectly.' Knowing God's will and fulfilling it: both elements are necessary in achieving authentic conversion.

LINKED BY AFFECTION

Ignatius relied greatly on his secretary, the Jesuit Polanco, to help him maintain the unity and growth of what Xavier called the 'Society of love'. He sent men off to distant places, alone and involved in risky undertakings, but he wanted to know their news and wanted them to share that news with one another. He once said he wanted to be informed even about the lice that were biting his sons. How much more, then, did he want to know of their labours, successes and failures. Receiving news brought him the greatest joy, especially when it was news from Xavier, who signed his letters 'your least son in the furthest exile'. Letters between them took two years to arrive. Xavier would read Ignatius's letter on his knees, and with tears. He treasured Ignatius's phrase: 'Completely yours, without my ever being able to forget you at any time, Ignatius.' He carried Ignatius's signature and those of his other distant companions in an amulet around his neck.

'The written word remains and is a witness for all times.'

Recall times when you were helped by others keeping in touch with you.

60. The Book that Changed the World

THE SPIRITUAL EXERCISES

If we were to ask Ignatius to reveal the secret of his extraordinary dynamism and the hidden source of so much generosity, without hesitation he would answer that this strength was a grace from God, which acts when we allow it to permeate us. For this grace to act, he had a formula, borne out both by his own experience and by his dealings with others, namely, the Spiritual Exercises. Ignatius has gone down in history as the author of this special formula whose effectiveness has been incalculable, from his time right down to the present and in every part of the world. Among the books that have changed the world, his *Spiritual Exercises* has a place of distinction, not merely because it has been translated into so many languages, but primarily because its message has been put into practice by millions of people. This little volume has gone through more than 4,500 editions, which averages one edition per month over the course of four centuries.

The book was composed to be lived, not read. Its success lies exclusively in the fact that it is so effective in what it sets out to do. Saint Francis de Sales used to say that this book produced more conversions than the sum total of all the letters used in writing it. It has been placed by a distinguished Protestant scholar, Heinrich Boehmer, among the books that have marked the destiny of humankind. An opponent of Ignatius such as Fülöp-Miller could describe the *Spiritual Exercises* as a book that brought about a complete revolution in Catholic thought, adding that there is no other work of Catholic literature that, in its historical effects, can be compared with it. It has received more than six hundred papal commendations as a very wise and universal code for directing souls. Writing to his former confessor in Paris, Ignatius himself said: 'The Spiritual Exercises are the best means that I can think, feel and understand in this life, both to help persons to benefit themselves and bring help, profit and advantage to many others.' Indeed, it is the very best of books.

PERSONAL EXPERIENCE

Before the Exercises were made into a book, however, they were Ignatius's personal experience, which began when he was convalescing at Loyola. He himself was the first exercitant. Later at Manresa, he sketched out the bare essentials of the Exercises, for his own personal use rather than for others. He then channelled his own experience and showed people how to open themselves so that they could hear God's personal invitation. In fact, he aroused suspicion because of the radical changes that took place in the lives of those who became his followers, for his early companions joined him as a result of having first made the Exercises. The book is a practical guide, not so much for the retreatant as for the guide or director, to be used like a manual that is employed to teach a pupil to play the piano or perform gymnastics. The Exercises can be judged only by those who have gone through them. The little book that became the spiritual basis of the Society of Jesus was approved even before the Constitutions of the Society were approved by popes.

GENEROUS HEARTS

Ignatius presupposes that the retreatant would have an open, generous and confident disposition. He asks the directee to withdraw from people and worldly cares and to keep silent. He leads him or her to liberation from obstacles that would hinder receptivity to God's call; then to a flowing tempo when the retreatant yields to the inspirations that come from God. The guide helps the retreatant to self-confrontation and to a response to God's calling. Reflection on the Word of God concludes in a conversation with God, and in the final offering of oneself: 'Take and receive, Lord, all my liberty, my understanding, all my will.' The God of Ignatius is not an abstract, distant being, but God revealed in Christ, who now works through the Spirit.

Ignatius was well aware of the blocks that could hinder people from coming to a right decision about what to do with their lives. The Exercises help to ensure authentic freedom 'to look for what I want'. Ignatius helps the exercitant to pass to a life that makes sense by provoking a personal awakening to Christ, since all that Christ did was done 'for me' personally. This encounter can have dramatic consequences. Believing that God is present in the soul of each person, he had confidence in each because he had confidence in the power of Christ's grace. He pressed for commitment – 'What should I do?' – convinced that it is in commitment that one finds God.

BECOMING NEW PERSONS

During Ignatius's lifetime, the full Exercises were given to some 7,500 persons, of whom about fifteen hundred were women, including religious, and about six thousand were men, of which number only approximately one thousand were already in religious life or became such afterward. Some were cardinals and bishops; the majority were lay men who continued on in their chosen state of life. For all, the Exercises meant an increase in religious fervour, a learning experience in personal prayer, a more significant and frequent reception of the sacraments, a radical spiritual conversion and a lasting reform of life, both personal and social. Many of these people described their personal experience graphically: they were born again in the Spirit; they became 'new persons'. Ignatius, toward the end of his life, noted that in addition to papal approval, the Exercises were also validated by the practical effects they brought about in people all over the world, 'people coming from all kinds of backgrounds and states of life'. And he added that any person of good will and free of passion who would make them would have the same experience.

The Exercises are a well of spirituality, valid for every age. The discipline, learning and experience that result from them represent not a momentary burst of religious enthusiasm but a method in one's continuous quest for God, in regenerated freedom, a way to give oneself to the Absolute, an attitude that can shape both fundamental choices as well as the minimal decisions of everyday life. Ignatius's immediate companions were living examples of their effectiveness, and Ignatius's entire life became the incarnation of his little book.

Reflect on your personal awakening to Christ and on its consequences.

61. Crafting the Jesuit Constitutions, 1540-51

GREATER SERVICE

While Ignatius sat in his little room in Rome, shaping the newly born Society, all was changing across Europe and the rest of the world. Religious and political divisions were everywhere, the Council of Trent ran from 1545 to 1563, the *Book of Common Prayer* was published in England, Xavier arrived in Japan, anti-slavery laws were passed for Latin America, and universities were established in Mexico city and in Lima. Everything was in turmoil, all was new. The changing scene was opening up paths for Ignatius that he had never before considered. He did not want to shut off such openings by being too hasty. 'In the meanwhile' was the expression he used for *ad hoc* solutions to immediate problems. Everything was watch and see, giving things time to clarify, experimenting and, all the while, not becoming frightened by the unexpected. How was he to incorporate in Constitutions the charism of the companions, and provide rules that would encapsulate their experiences and better define their mission? He was not in a hurry to find the answer, but he never stopped working at it. In the meantime, he had the task of governing the living Society. All of this activity gives us an insight into his immense talent as an organiser. He was doing everything at the same time, giving himself completely to each project in turn. The preferred fields of action of the Society, enshrined in Part VII of the Constitutions, are born of reflection on what was happening to the early members: the *greater service* of God; where there is *greater need* or more danger; where the door is more widely open, where there is hope of *greater fruit*, where there is *greater universal good*, etc. All of this had to be translated into the choice of the best qualified persons to fulfil specific tasks.

BORN OF EXPERIENCE

As deliberate as a sculptor, Ignatius slowly chiselled the cornerstones upon which he would later build the Constitutions. Polanco, his secretary from 1547 onward, served him well by studying the rules of other orders. Thus the profile of the Society gradually emerged, and in 1550 Pope Julius III issued a new bull sanctioning the changes that experience had imposed on earlier documents. The moulds were now set that would last for centuries. The purpose of the Society was now spelled out as the defence and the propagation of the faith. After the comments of the early companions had been incorporated in 1552, Ignatius entrusted Nadal with the task of making the Constitutions known and putting them into practice. He remained open, however, to the demands of experience, for he always allowed himself to be taught by life. One must read between the lines of the Constitutions to discover there, as in a watermark, the image of Ignatius's plan of action, his way, the heart of the Exercises – in short, the most profound part of his personality. Life lived and history experienced are enshrined in these laws. They are written in the spirit of a man of action and are the fruit of much prayer, reflection and lessons learnt from daily experience. They move from grand ideals to minute details, because Ignatius realised that an insignificant leak could destroy a roof, that it is through the tiniest apertures that the most precious liquid is lost: as the Spanish proverb has it, gigantic mud pits are formed from specks of dust.

Ignatius wrote a great part of the Constitutions seated at a small table in the garden. Here he listened to the voice within and reflected on his own ideals and personal experience. The Constitutions are more a mould than a cold law. He did not want them to oblige under pain of sin: rather 'It is the interior law of charity and love that the Holy Spirit writes and engraves on hearts that should help us, more than any exterior constitution'. In Part IX, Ignatius speaks of the kind of person the superior general should be: it is an unconscious self-portrait. He should be closely united with God our Lord and intimate with God in prayer and in all that he does, so that he can be a source of inspiration for all. He ought to love others and be truly humble, be master of his passions, and show magnanimity and fortitude so that he can bear the weaknesses of others, and take on great projects without losing courage in the face of contradictions.

UNIVERSAL LOVE

In the final part of the Constitutions, described as his last will and testament, he expresses his most intimate conviction, the staunch belief of the onetime pilgrim who had placed his hope in God alone: 'Because the Society was not instituted by human means, it is not through them that it can be preserved and developed, but rather through the all-powerful hand of Christ, our God and our Lord. Therefore, in him alone must be placed the hope that he will preserve and carry forward what he deigned to begin for his service and praise and for the aid of souls.' The basic law for Ignatius was as follows: 'Live always in love and with charity for all ... a universal love that embraces everyone.' Through the Constitutions, Ignatius formed a community whose destiny it was to realise an ideal. He broke with the historic culture of his time by turning his back on wealth, by introducing a fraternal spirit between people whose countries were at war with one another, by encouraging persons to make a gift of themselves for the service of God and the peoples of five different continents. He made courage a bonus and hard work a premium, and encouraged his followers to accept humbly that while waging battle in the hearts of all, and winning them over one by one, they would be the objects of unproductive criticism and negativity.

'He should be closely united with God and intimate with God in prayer and in all that he does.'

How far have you grown in intimacy with God in prayer and in what you do?

62. Resignation Refused, 1551

TOTAL OBSTACLE?

Action was Ignatius's expression of hope in a Europe that was living without hope, crushed as it was by black forebodings and fatalism. But Ignatius was not the ordinary man of action, trusting in his own resources and leadership. Rather than being an actor, he felt acted upon and he did not believe in his own self-sufficiency. His action generated energy because it left aside the attitude of 'How can I be self-fulfilled'? He had a strong sense of his own spiritual poverty, and stated in a letter: 'I am a total obstacle.' By this he meant that he was insensitive to much of what God wanted to do in him. Is this the pious exaggeration of a saint? Such an interpretation is most comfortable for us to accept. But, in reality, it corresponds to something very deeply rooted in his spirit, and underlines the tremendous distance that he saw between his own self and the extraordinary fruitfulness of his life.

NOT SO POORLY

In 1551, Ignatius tried to resign from the generalship. This decision was not the result of some momentary discouragement. Perhaps he felt too old for the job at sixty, and during the previous year he had serious health problems. More likely, his decision was inspired by the realisation that he had accomplished what he had set out to do: the Constitutions were written, and the Society and the Spiritual Exercises had been approved. Perhaps his companions did not realise the intensity that Ignatius had put into the document of resignation that he submitted to them, and that he had meditated on each sentence at length in silence. Even to this day, these sentences cannot be read without emotion: 'After having thought about and considered it for years without any inner or outer disturbance, I shall say before my Creator and Lord, who is to judge me for all eternity, what I feel and understand is to be for the greater praise and glory of His Divine Majesty. Looking realistically into myself, and taking into account my many sins, my imperfections, and my numerous illnesses … I have come to the conclusion, many times and on different occasions, that I do not have the qualities required to take charge of the Society.... I wish that this be carefully considered in the Lord and that another should be elected, who could do this work better or not so poorly as myself.... I simply and absolutely give up the charge I now have, asking and praying with all my soul in the Lord, that the professed, as well as those who will join them in deciding upon it, may accept my request....'

Ignatius was convinced that God had inspired his wish. But also, he had long decided not to be his own master and not to determine his own life. Through the mouths of those who had gathered in Rome in 1551, and who refused his request, God spoke to him and opposed his most fervent desire. And therefore he remained on as general to the very end, while not completely resigned to the fact, but giving himself, body and soul, to his work, and energetically undertaking new and important enterprises.

AMBITIOUS PLANS

Thus, during the final five years of his life, Ignatius consolidated existing activities and initiated new ones. The Jesuit Colleges, originally founded for Jesuit students, were opened to lay persons and were free of charge, and the characteristics of Jesuit education began to emerge. Ignatius had no modern organisational charts to rely on, nor did he have our means of communication, but this in no way prevented him from responding to the heartbeat of the whole world. His creativity was channelled by ambitious plans, which he undertook after consideration and prudent advice. He was very much the realist in his endeavours. In 1551 and 1552, he began two undertakings that were destined to make their presence felt down through the centuries: the Roman College, which became the present-day Gregorian University, the most prestigious university in the Christian world, and the German College, founded to form priests for Central Europe. He placed men in various universities across Europe and he drew up a plan to reform the University of Vienna.

SMALL LIGHTS EVERYWHERE

Ignatius tried to promote the faith in those places where Christianity had never been introduced, and in places compromised by religious divisions or infected by the spirit of decadence. He did not complain about the darkness of the age, but lit small lights everywhere. He established projects in the Congo, Ethiopia, Brazil, India and Japan. With only a handful of men, he tried to raise the Church in Germany from the ruins brought about by the Reformation. The first objective was to regain Germany for the Catholic Church and the second was to establish the Society there. In 1549, he gave the Jesuits who were working on this mission precise and prudent instructions. They were to have complete confidence in God; they were to pray, give example by their lives, show sincere love to all, and adapt themselves to all. They must have an exact knowledge of the people they would be dealing with, and work in teams. They would give public lectures, instruct and exhort, hear confessions, attract young men who could be their co-workers in the future, give the full thirty-day Exercises, and visit prisoners, the sick and the poor. They were to become friendly with the leaders of the heretics, in order to elucidate controversial dogmatic points, and to treat all persons 'with love, desire for their wellbeing, and more than anything else, with compassion'.

DETERMINATION

Once Ignatius had decided that a particular project was worthwhile, nothing or no one could deter him from carrying it through. A single anecdote will illustrate this. In November 1552, Ignatius was on the point of leaving Rome in order to help to save a marriage that was floundering. Just as he was about to leave the house, the rain came down in torrents. Everyone wanted him to put off the excursion, but his answer was a veritable self-portrait: 'We are leaving right now, because in thirty years I have never altered the time I had fixed to do something in God's service because of rain, wind or any other weather problem.' His mission failed, but he addressed the people in two villages on the way and organised in them the practice of monthly Communion. He never took a step without leaving the trace of his footprint behind.

63. 'The sad misery of this life', 1553

STILL ALIVE

Ignatius showed extraordinary energy in governing the Society of Jesus from 1540 to 1556. This, however, did not stem from natural enthusiasm or rare biological energy in an ageing man. In early 1552, he wrote to Francis Xavier describing what life was like for him, as something he had now to put up with rather than what he had enjoyed in the energy of youth. His fine script was a way in which he could show his distant friend that he could still move his hand and control his pen 'to let you know that I am still alive amidst the sad misery of this life'. But this sad misery was not the same thing as lack of spirit, indolence, an excuse to neglect work, or being forlorn, for in a covering letter from Polanco, Ignatius brings Xavier up to date on a multitude of Jesuit projects across Europe. The pressure of them all renders more human his comment about the sad misery of life.

Curiously, on the very same day that Ignatius was writing from Rome, 31 January 1552, Xavier was writing from Cochin a long account of his own adventures, which were also rich in worries and filled with the sadness of life. 'I am covered with grey hair … and on this I finish.' He expresses his wish to see Ignatius again in this life, and suggests that an order from Ignatius could bring the two together again. Xavier also was suffering from weariness of life, although he, too, kept on working as hard as ever. This fact is seen in his last letter, written just a few days before he died. 'If it is God's will I shall not die, although in times past I have had a greater desire to live than I do now….' At the same time, he spoke with unrestrained passion of Japan, China and India, and asked for the support of 'persons who have the courage to do much and in many places'. Ignatius finally ordered him back to Europe, but the anxiously awaited summons arrived only after Xavier's death, a death Ignatius did not learn about until two years afterward. The news caused Ignatius great pain, a pain that was added to many other sufferings and tribulations.

FRUSTRATIONS

Ignatius knew frustrations during his later years, but he bore them peacefully and in silence. Disputes with families whose sons had joined the Society without the expressed consent of their parents gave him concern. More troublesome were the problems that resulted from distrust of the local Jesuit

College by the Republic of Venice. Teachers from other institutions, faced with competition from the new College, resorted to spreading lies, throwing stones and causing violent interruptions in the classes of the new school. However, the most serious demonstrations against the Jesuit schools took place in Rome itself. The sign announcing the opening day of the Roman College read: 'School of Grammar, Humanities and Christian Doctrine. Gratis.' On the surface, the basis for disagreement was concern about the College's academic credentials, but in reality it was the word Gratis (free of charge) that was the cause of opposition. The quality of teaching was guaranteed by the teaching structure that the Jesuits implemented – an academic plan that soon caused a revolution in teaching methods throughout Italy. The Roman College met with overnight success for a number of reasons, including the addition of classes in rhetoric, philosophy and theology. Then there were the public debates, which cardinals came to witness. The pope was quick to give the College the right to grant diplomas, while more and more well-selected masters began to appear in its lecture halls. Finally, thanks to ever-increasing enrolments, the College had to move to a new and more functional building.

HEROIC TASKS

The precarious finances of the Roman College gave Ignatius any number of nightmares. This tuition-free institution was founded without a single cent of endowment, but, thanks to the generosity of Francis Borgia and the alms given by Pope Julius III, it did manage to stay afloat. Ignatius always had to find strength in his own weakness in order to take on difficult and heroic undertakings, and he had to rely more on God than on human beings. In this case, his debt was in excess of seventy thousand ducats, and he was not able even to pay the interest on the loans received. There were times when the days of the Roman College appeared to be numbered, and when it seemed that Ignatius would end up in prison. Although such dire consequences never came about, the Roman Jesuits had to tighten their belts and be content with seeing their daily ration of meat cut in half and with having one egg apiece on Fridays and Saturdays. The famous Roman College would not know economic stability until Gregory XIII endowed it generously, hence the title of Gregorian University, but that did not happen until 1581, twenty-five years after the death of Ignatius. Likewise, chronic economic crises were played out for the German College, which was so vital for Catholic reform in Central Europe. The spectre of bankruptcy was always on the horizon.

DISOBEDIENCE

Another problem must have been the disobedience and stubbornness of Simon Rodrigues, one of the founding fathers with a mercurial temperament.

He was impulsive, independent and very attached to his native land of Portugal and to the pleasant company of its nobles at the court. He disobeyed orders and spoke ill of Ignatius, who finally wrote him a sensitive personal letter, encouraging him to come to Rome. In a famous letter on obedience written to the Society in Portugal in March 1553, he lists the consequences of failing to maintain obedience: pain, discontent, weariness, complaints, excuses and other faults. Ignatius wanted a spontaneous obedience coming from the interior of a person. Older religious orders might surpass the Society in penances, in the liturgy of the hours and the singing of the office in choir, but none should surpass the Society in obedience. In late 1553, Rodrigues arrived in Rome and was finally ordered to leave Portugal, but he carried on his intrigues from Rome. His endless requests to return home were granted only in 1574, and he died there five years later.

Xavier asked for the support of persons who have the courage to do much.

Do you find in yourself the courage to do much, or do you at least wish for it?

64. 'What could make me sad', 1554

ATTACKED

Besides his concerns about certain members of the Society, Ignatius had worries that came from outside, the most damaging being incessant attacks from some Dominicans. They accused him of being a heretic who had fled to Rome to escape the Inquisition. The very name 'Society of Jesus' was denounced as proud and schismatic. Then, in 1553, the theological faculty of Paris University issued a remarkable decree that attacked the Society head-on. The Society was castigated for its name, for the fact that Jesuits wore no religious habit and for its ecclesiastical privileges. Further, it was alleged, it posed a danger to the faith, disturbed peace within the Church, was poisonous to other religious orders and was composed of individuals who were born to destroy rather than build, given that some of its members were illegitimate while others were criminals.

Ignatius did not lose his peace and tranquillity in this terrible tempest. He respected the decree and forbade anyone to contradict it. He wanted to reply only to the suspicions and lies it contained, so he sought qualified testimony from those who knew the Society, an excellent example of his style of acting. 'Write to all Jesuits throughout the whole Society *today straight away*,' he said to Polanco, 'and tell them that they should begin sending testimonies from princes, governors, universities, from wherever the colleges are, from every Province.' An impressive harvest of praises was collected, but to no avail. Some of his supporters considered drafting a pontifical bull of excommunication against the enemies of the Society, but Ignatius refused, out of respect and love for the University of Paris, 'which was the mother of the first members of the Society'. The charges were never withdrawn, and Ignatius would die with this thorn in his heart. He had endured the first of many furious attacks against the Society that would be launched throughout the centuries.

CARAFA ELECTED

The most painful trial of all for Ignatius, who was a most faithful servant of the papacy, was in a totally different category. He had enjoyed the support of Paul III and Julius III, and then of Marcellus II, who died of a heart attack after three weeks in office, having asked Ignatius for two theologians to help him in reforming the Church. Ignatius's fear was that Cardinal Carafa would now be elected. This Carafa had spread rumours about Ignatius throughout Venice, had brought him to the attention of the Inquisition, had never supported Ignatius in Rome, and believed that the Society should not be exempt from choir. Ignatius believed very deeply in divine providence, but this fact did not stop him from paying attention to human affairs. A few years earlier, perhaps during one of his health crises, his doctor had ordered him to avoid anything that could cause melancholy, or depression as we would name it today. There was only one thing, it seems, that could sadden that robust personality: in conversation with Câmara, to whom he dictated his *Autobiography,* he said: 'I have been thinking about what could cause me melancholy, and I found that there was only one thing – if the pope were completely to disband the Society. And even in this case I think that if I were to recollect myself in prayer for a quarter of an hour, I would be as happy as before.' He asked his men to pray 'that if it be to the equal service of God, there will not be elected a pope who will make changes to what pertains to the Society, for there are some among the candidates about whom there is fear that they would make such changes'. When he received news in May 1554 that Carafa was elected, Ignatius could not hold back his feelings. His face visibly changed and his body trembled. He got up from his seat and went to pray in the chapel. A few minutes later, he returned, his face transformed and serene, accepting completely what could not be changed.

DARK NIGHT

Ignatius asked the Society to pray for the new pope, about whom he said, perhaps too generously: 'He has always been a friend of the Society.' Earlier popes had approved the 'way' of the Society, which seemed to have been mapped out by divine providence. Now the axis of unconditional self-surrender to the pope, around which the Society revolved, was grinding under the changes that Paul IV could set into motion. For Ignatius, this was the dark night of faith, the purification of hope, his total abandonment to the designs of God. He maintained his fidelity and lived out his rules about 'feeling with the Church' in a stark, uncomfortable way, but with patience. He was being taught the tension between institution and charism, between the voice of authority and the strength of the voice of God.

In reality, all of this was an intimate, hidden drama, because things were not as bad on the surface as Ignatius had feared. Carafa met with him and other Jesuits, though he did not give Ignatius a single cent to relieve his desperate financial situation. His suspicions of the Jesuits led him also to order a humiliating search for non-existent arms in the Jesuit house where Ignatius lived. He later forced some Jesuits to work in reinforcing the defences of

'Only one thing could cause me melancholy – if the pope were to disband the Society.'

Rome, in preparation for an absurd war against Spain. Ignatius never spoke a word against him. One day, however, a revealing sentence escaped his lips. The pope, he said, 'could reform the world if he could first change himself, his household, his curia, and the city of Rome.' When Ignatius lay dying, he asked for the pope's blessing. Shortly after Ignatius's death, the pope revealed his hidden feelings about what he claimed was the tyrannical domination of Ignatius over the Society. Henceforth, he ruled, the Jesuits would recite the divine office in choir and the General would serve for three years only. It was in this glacial and stormy atmosphere that the life of Ignatius, the papacy's supremely faithful servant, came to an end. Added to his everyday concerns, to the weariness of never-ending correspondence, worries about mounting debts and the rising cost of living, the fatigue of dealing with budding hostilities and new enterprises, the distress caused by seeing his men threatened with expulsion in some places – to all of these was added this deepest and all-embracing suffering, that which followed the election of Paul IV.

How do you respond to distressing situations and the shattering of your dreams?

65. Physical Decline, 1554-56

WORN DOWN

Although Ignatius continued his hands-on policy in all administrative affairs, he did not have the strength he once had, and he spent most of 1554 in bed. Nadal was appointed vicar-general. The following year he felt better and put his signature on more than a thousand letters. He governed the Society in all its details. He dreamt of founding one College in Prague and another in Mexico, of establishing an Arab College in Palermo and others in Cyprus, Constantinople and Jerusalem. He was endlessly imaginative. Without his being aware of it, his men tried to free him from his labours. They limited the number of visitors he received; they filtered out from the news any matters that would worry him; and they surrounded him with the care befitting a man suffering from persistent fatigue. The doctor told him to take more exercise and counselled him against the bad consequences of 'deep thinking, especially vivid spiritual or temporal imaginings', which was perfectly useless advice. The doctor also recommended nutritious food for his chronic cold and stomach pains. But Ignatius would only eat breadcrumbs, just to show that he was eating, and when a small glass of sweet wine was prepared for him he would taste it and then give it to someone else and say, 'Here, you're in poorer shape than I.' He slept little; he would pace up and down in his cell, thinking, praying and working. As a remedy for his worries, he would sometimes get away from his workplace. Ribadeneira tells us about this: 'He would go to the terrace or to a place where all the heavens were visible. There he would stand, take off his cap, and remain still for a short while with his eyes lifted towards the sky. Then he would kneel and bow down before God; afterward he would sit down on a low bench because the weakness of his body did not permit him to do anything else. Here he would sit with his head uncovered and with tears streaming ever so gently and silently that one heard not a single sigh or any rustling whatsoever.' Although music soothed him and eased his cares, he used it only rarely. One human pleasure, humble and touching, is recorded: 'Sometimes the greatest thing that we could do for him was to give him four roasted chestnuts, which, because they were a fruit of his native land, seemed to give him pleasure.'

LEGACY

The essentials were now complete: the approbation of the Society, the Spiritual Exercises and the Constitutions. In 1555, Ignatius then satisfied the request of his companions by revealing the intimacy of his soul in the autobiographical account that he dictated to Câmara. When Nadal was leaving Rome that same year, he recommended that people should not tire Ignatius: 'The thing that we must be most concerned with is that our father should have rest' so that he might enjoy himself in the vineyard or in some other place. Nadal knew that this leisure was neither laziness nor wool-gathering, but something active and effective: 'His leisure moments, since he is so familiar and united to God, nourish and support the whole Society.'

HIDDEN LIFE

Viewed from outside, Ignatius's life at this point seems to have been simple, monotonous and retiring. Over a period of fifteen years, from 1541 to 1556, he left Rome only five times, and yet the whole world came to his cell in the form of letters, news items and projects planned. His early Roman apostolic activities soon gave way to the business of administration and to the direction of souls. He lived a life hidden behind his correspondence and papers, retired within himself, but ever active; he was taken out of his solitude by travelling Jesuits who would come and go; for hours and hours his faithful secretary Polanco walked alongside him. He had his cell in which he slept, a small room in which he worked, and an adjacent dining room where he would be joined by Jesuits passing through Rome, superiors of the Society, or guests 'who wanted to do penance' at his table. He loved poverty in everything, but also order and cleanliness. There was something courtly and noble about the way he received his guests, but it was more in his manners than in the fare he offered. He wore a simple cassock and fought the cold with a large coat. In the house, he used a cane. It was impressive to see him walking in the house, or on the street going to some specific place or to see some particular person. The fair hair of his youth had long since disappeared; he was bald and wore a short beard, above which loomed an aquiline nose and high cheekbones. His complexion had become darker, perhaps even yellowish because of his liver ailment. His countenance, serious and peaceful, was the image of circumspection and of a life lived interiorly; some found it particularly luminous and expressive. His eyes, once sparkling bright, were now blurred by work, old age and copious tears; they had lost their gaiety but not their penetrating force. His gaze had the power of seeing straight through a person, right to the heart.

GOOD LISTENER

Ignatius was not a bookish man; however, he kept the *Imitation of Christ* by Thomas à Kempis beside him. He was not an intellectual, not even a serious scholar. He had no interest in religious speculation nor did he like controversy. He preferred to affirm people, and he refused to believe gossip about others: he never criticised anyone and he excused their faults. His strength was in word and in action. What interested him were individual human beings, personal problems, concrete things. He relied more on experience than on books. Though he was never a great preacher or a professor, the naked, clear word, endowed with an enormous strength, was his greatest weapon. He spoke little, and always after much reflection. He never exaggerated nor uttered an unnecessary word. He made conversation an art, and would listen with all his being, sometimes asking questions. Thus he would establish a total transparency with the other person. He was a master of intimate conversation, and left an indelible mark on those who entered into authentic communication with him.

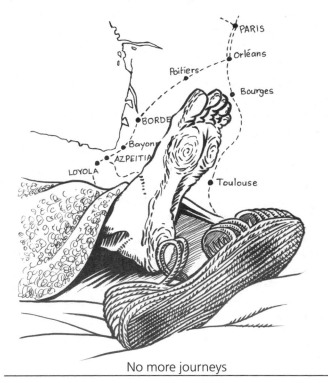

No more journeys

Ignatius refused to believe gossip about others, and he never criticised anyone.

How do you respond to hearing negative gossip about others?

66. 'He seemed to be all love'

PATIENT AND ACTIVE

For Ignatius, the mechanisms of coming to a decision were complex. He would always thoroughly think out a problem before he made up his mind, and then he would follow up on it irrespective of the consequences. His bulldog tenacity in matters small and great was legendary. 'Whenever he makes up his mind that something is to be done, he has so much faith in it that he acts as if it were already done.' He had faith in action, in commitment. He was both patient and active. He was able to wait in a cardinal's empty chamber a whole day without eating; he was a believer in providence and at the same time he was thoroughly rational. The difficult or the impossible never frightened him. Mature consideration and tenacity of purpose were his secret weapons. First, he was successful in the battle over himself, and afterward he was successful with others: 'He never undertook a thing he did not finish, and he did not allow himself to be easily defeated.' Fighting battles and facing adversaries fortified him and reinvigorated his precarious and failing health. He firmly believed that where there are many contradictions, one should expect a great spiritual harvest. He bore his trials without complaint. At Loyola, he had twice endured the surgeon's butchery for a whole day; in his later life, he put up with recurrent gallstone attacks. He also endured in silence the spiritual sufferings that resulted from observing the moral decadence of the Church of his time.

RADIANT SERENITY

Those around Ignatius admired his radiant serenity, his equanimity. Although by nature fiery and aggressive, he seemed now to be imperturbable. It was not that he was insensitive, but he was always even-tempered. The ups and downs of his health did not affect this serenity, no matter what the circumstances were. 'In order to obtain something from our father,' observed Ribadeneira, 'it was the same thing to approach him after he had finished saying his Mass or when he was eating, when he got up from his bed or after he had learned good or bad news, and it made no difference if the world was at peace or consigned to destruction. And so no one needed to guess what he was thinking, as one must usually do when dealing with those who govern, because he was always imperturbable and master of himself.'

'ALL LEFT SMILING'

Ignatius was respected, venerated, but, most especially, he was loved: he inspired trust, confidence and freedom. Though not all might agree, one witness stated: 'All who left his little room left comforted and smiling.' He was very exacting, beginning with himself, but infinitely more flexible with others than is usually believed. According to Câmara: 'He seemed to be all love. He is universally loved by everyone. I know no one in this Society who does not have a great love for him and does not think that he is very greatly loved by the father.' In March 1555, while he was telling Câmara how at one time he would pray long hours and perform terrible penances, he added that now 'it seemed to him that there was no greater mistake in spiritual matters than wishing to govern others as one rules oneself'. He knew that not everyone was a spiritual giant, but he did train some to become just that, and he gave to all the desire to surpass what they thought was their capacity. Laínez, Polanco and Nadal, for instance, suffered tough treatment from Ignatius, and often asked God what sins they had committed that such a saint would treat them so. While Ignatius was uncompromising about obedience, he preferred to suggest rather than to order; he wanted everything to be done generously and with gladness of heart, without obedience explicitly being invoked. When he had to turn down a permission, he preferred someone else to communicate this, but if he had to do it himself, he liked to explain the reasons why the request was denied and 'he shows so much love that all who leave him with a "no" are quite happy, and all the things that he says are well-grounded so that the person accepts fully what he says'. He possessed the secret of the art of commanding. While he seemed to control everything, he gave provincials and those on special missions all possible personal responsibility, and he wanted them to use it, keeping in mind this principle: 'Show love and consider the universal good.'

Was there some hidden shyness in the soul of Ignatius that would explain all of these things? Câmara stated that Ignatius was affable toward all, but intimate with none. Was this the loneliness of the leader? He was affable and communicative; he could talk about his personal experiences; he sought out help and persons to guide him, but he was undemonstrative and manifested his feelings rarely, and then only in the strictest confidence. He had an immense, hidden inner world, impregnable, jealously guarded: in studying him, we must distinguish his nature from what he made out of it, or better, how he chiselled and conquered it.

A GREAT MIND

We get some insight into Ignatius's personality through the secret gallery of his handwriting. He had a neat, strong, down-to-earth hand, which wrote

He radiated respect, solicitude and love for others.

with the precision of a sculptor, manifesting a mind that was methodical, orderly and clear. What is striking about his writing as a whole is that he was true to himself, to who and what he was, from the very beginning to the end of his life. His initial aggressiveness had been channelled over a lifetime: this was a decisive conquest in which he was aided by his ability to withdraw into himself, to contemplate, and to listen attentively and carefully to an inner presence deep within his being. His writing denotes greatness and nobility of soul; a confident progression toward the future, troubled neither by fear nor illness; the realisation of an inner harmony. He projects great security. The largeness of his field of consciousness propelled him to take on great undertakings. The heart of Ignatius – a heart so enigmatic and controlled – sings in his writings, and here he wears no protecting mask. He was a well of goodness, understanding, affectivity, compassion; he radiated courteous respect, solicitude and tender love for others.

Do people experience respect, solicitude and love from you?

67. Finding God in All Things

SENSITIVITY TO GOD

While psychology can help us to understand Ignatius, his total personality would be unintelligible if reduced to sheer psychological analysis. Genuine sincerity is one of the dominant characteristics of Ignatius, who always wanted to be authentic and who never gave in to a sterile and inactive introspection. His sincerity goes hand in hand with the will to be transformed; in the words of Louis Lavelle, it is 'a need to entrust oneself to impulses in which the "I" is forgotten and one lets oneself be guided by superior forces'. Ignatius recognised and felt the presence of an all-surrounding, fundamental reality, which is God, manifested in Christ. An introvert, he found in himself something that went beyond himself. His authenticity, his freedom, made him the captive of truth in mind and heart. He was a mystic, a saint, always attentive to the 'rumours of angels' that he perceived in the very depth of his soul. He passionately sought an ultimate transparency, an unconditional flexibility in the hands of a superior agent who pushed him on, not by words but by actions, toward a future that remained for a long time uncertain. He was a perpetual, sensitive listener to the Word of God, to an internal Word strengthened by joy and peace, more than by the written word found in the Bible – a rarely found attitude.

MYSTICAL AWARENESS

Those around Ignatius detected a profound mystery in his soul. From time to time, he let some intimate detail of this mystery escape, either in the pages of his *Spiritual Journal* or in his *Autobiography*. A reserved, discreet man, he spoke with greater ease about his old sins than he did about his interior illuminations. He died without revealing the secret of 'a certain thing that happened in Manresa', and without really telling us about his visions, his mystical conversations, and the ultimate reason for all those tears that ruined his eyes, tears that he shed while at prayer or saying Mass. He would have agreed with the Austrian philosopher Wittgenstein, who stated: 'It is better to be silent about the things one cannot speak about.' And silent he remained about his interior life. Yet everyone knew that celebrating Mass was an experience that tested his physical strength and health. He did not have the physical strength to celebrate daily, because of the 'vehement commotion' that took place within him, and he became ill whenever he did. The Mass, which for so many is a routine religious function, was a singular event for Ignatius, a privileged moment for his intimate mystical experiences. We get a glimpse of these, if no more than a peek, when reading the *Spiritual Journal,* which he wrote in his laconic style.

HE FOLLOWED THE SPIRIT

Ignatius found God not only at Mass and in quiet prayer, but also in the confused messiness of his daily work, with all its problems and concerns, and in conversations with others. The objective that Ignatius proposed to his followers, 'to find God in all things', constituted his own inner attitude. Nadal got to the heart of it when he said: 'He followed the Spirit who led him, he did not go before the Spirit.' Rather than being a leader, Ignatius was basically someone who was always being led, led by God. In this autumn of his life, a secret escaped his lips, a confidence that is typical of mystics: he said that his way was more passive than active. The proverbial man of action, therefore, was a man acted upon, more receptive than active, although he appeared the opposite to many who observed him. In his notes of 1555, Câmara insists on this same notion in an imaginative and elementary way: 'Whatever the father does for God, he does it with wonderful recollection and promptitude, and it seems that not only does he imagine he has God before him, it seems that he sees God with his eyes and one can notice this in the way he says grace at the table....'

During those long hours of reflective meditation, and during those moments of retrospection that his quiet, hidden life fostered, Ignatius must have reflected upon the curve of his life's arch and on his work in much the same way, that is, *as one who was led.* If he were to look back on his life when close to dying, the weary general of the Society could contemplate the fruit of only fifteen years of governing. From the nine original companions, the Society now numbered almost a thousand. They were spread out across the world in some eighty houses. They were divided into fourteen provinces and were working in the most varied ministries. Had he been able to foresee the future, he would have been surprised that eighteen years later the Society would have multiplied fourfold to more than four thousand Jesuits. By the year 1600, forty-four years after his death, it had doubled again to more than eight thousand. Astonishment rather than pride would have been his reaction.

GOD LEADING THE SOCIETY

Ignatius seems to have had contradictory views in regard to the astonishing growth of the Society of Jesus. On the one hand, he worried that the later generation of Jesuits were not as heroic as the first. Once, thinking about the Paris days – something he did quite often – he remembered how rigorously the companions as a group had made the Exercises for the first time. They shut themselves off from everything and everyone, they fasted, put up with severe cold and performed many penances. This prompted him to make the rather excessive judgement: 'But now, all of that means nothing [to this new generation of Jesuits].' On the other hand, he found encouragement in the generosity of the young, and he recognised the extent to which the improvisations of the past had influenced the present. And so he said: 'The ones who will come will be better and will do more, because of our stumbling along.' As he looked toward the future, Ignatius had a 'treasury of hopes' that was greater than the realities of the developing Society. He was deeply convinced that God was leading the Society 'as if it were a thing of his own'.

Ignatius was a perpetual, sensitive listener to the internal Word of God.

Do you listen to the Word of God spoken in your heart?

68. 'If I followed my own inclinations'

LOVER OF MUSIC

Ignatius indeed had a deep conviction that God was leading the Society, and this meant that he would sometimes be led where he had no wish to go, as the risen Jesus warned Peter at the lakeside (John 21:18). As a symbol of this side of his history, one aspect can be singled out – music. Ignatius loved music, and one of his relatives stated categorically of the younger Ignatius: 'He was a musician, but he never played on Fridays or Saturdays.' Câmara stated of him a few years before his death: 'If there was one thing that transported him in prayer, it was the music and chant of Mass and Vespers; and so much so, that as he told me himself, if he heard the singing of the divine office, he was completely transported out of himself. This was not only for the good of his soul, but also for his bodily health.' In his *Spiritual Journal,* Ignatius tells us that the summit of divine consolation for him took the form of a vibration, a heavenly music, perceived both interiorly and exteriorly. It appears that the most vivid impression of the Lord's presence in his heart was modulated in sound.

THE LORD HIS GUIDE

Why then did Ignatius eliminate the obligation of choir from his Order? It was to ensure that Jesuit life would be flexible, so that his men could go wherever they were needed and find God in all things. Ribadeneira recounts that in 1554, when hearing music in the Church of Saint Joseph, Ignatius stated: 'If I had followed my own taste and inclinations, I would have introduced choir and chant in the Society, but I did not do so because God our Lord let me understand that it was not his will, and he does not want us to serve him in choir but by doing other things in his service.' '*If I followed my own taste and inclinations....*' Here is a key to his life, which was like a ceaseless conversation, and his entire part in this conversation was an act of subordination. To all appearances, he was in no way under the obedience of anyone, for he was a man born to lead and guide others. But his whole life was an act of heroic submission to the divine will, which at times seemed so disconcerting. Other than in matters of ecclesiastical obedience, 'the Lord was his only guide' (Deuteronomy 32:12). Ignatius becomes understandable only in the light of this fact. The master of his life was not himself; it was Another.

This is why his personal history is a chain of unfulfilled desires, of unexpected results, a surprising mixture of death and life, a succession of 'burned ships' and circuitous meanderings.

TRANSFORMED DESIRES

To summarise: the pride, lust and desire for power of his lineage had died in him many years before. The lady of his dreams, his desire to go back to the world, his plans to enter the Carthusians and lead a hidden life, all of these had long since been abandoned. He was no longer tempted to extreme penances or to surpassing the deeds of the saints. Later, there were more subtle forms of renunciation, frustration of noble and legitimate desires, dreams and projects. For a long time, he did not think of founding an Order, but he became the head of the most organised and modern Order of all. He had thought of surrounding himself with a handful of men, but they multiplied like grass on the plains. He wanted a hidden, anonymous life, but he became prestigious, well known, and he saw his companions spread throughout the whole world. He had liked dusty roads, hospices that catered to travellers, simple people, and he ended up visiting palaces, surrounded by academics and corresponding with cardinals and kings. The resolute pilgrim had become the most immobile and sedentary of men. The pilgrim's spirit had become an organisational spirit.

Ignatius had wanted to obey, but he was saddled with giving orders and directions. He was most submissive to the hierarchical Church, but he appeared to be a silent, effective rebel against many of the Church's laws and regulations. He had been a kind of free-spirited spiritual vagabond, and he finished up dictating Constitutions and interminable rules. His simplicity and spiritual spontaneity appeared to have been transformed into a complicated system of organisational norms. Everyone thought that he was a masterful planner, but only he knew to what extent he had listened to the Holy Spirit, the signs of the times, and diverse circumstances. His roots were burrowed deep in the soil of the Middle Ages, and yet he was the very incarnation of innovation and modernity. Driven by the desire to catechise children and illiterate people, he founded and supported colleges and universities for the élite. Some have thought him totally immersed in his own egocentricity, whereas he had handed over his soul to Another: 'Take, Lord, and receive all my liberty, my memory, my understanding, and my entire will, all that I have and possess.' And, as we have stressed often before, to top off all of these contradictions, Ignatius had been tenacious in believing that God was calling him to live in Jerusalem; yet God led him to Rome.

Ignatius had given himself over to Another in love.

ADORATION

What if Ignatius had died at Pamplona? What if there had been only books on knight-errantry at Loyola? What if he had drowned during his trip to Palestine or been killed at the hands of the French on his way to Paris? What if there had been a pilgrim ship available to take him and his first companions to Jerusalem? What if Paul III had not invited the companions to his Roman dinner table or had denied their first requests? Events could have been otherwise, but in fact Ignatius followed the itinerary of Another, driving forward, in the later words of Saint John of the Cross, 'without any other light or guide save that which was burning in his heart'. He was a profound believer, an integrated man at peace with himself, and therefore he was able to accept whatever came along. He had given himself over to Another in love. Loyola, the indefatigable man of action, was a tireless man of prayer, a man who adored God at all times.

'Giving yourself over to Another in love' – Does this describe the movement of your life?

69. The Quiet Reformer

ORIGINALITY

Ignatius lived during a muddled period of history that was passionate, heroic, torn apart, and rich in the names of the men and women who left their imprint on the history of western civilisation. In his youth, he had been indistinguishable from any other European; he became different, original and even singular only after he 'stopped to think', and this led him to cross an invisible frontier, which the majority of the human race never crosses. Then he started on his way; in part it was a very old way, but it was also a personal and new way, like those small, all but imperceptible paths that the beasts create along the mountainside in his native land. With a blind faith in the future, with the faith of another Abraham, he left his own country and followed this little pathway, uncertain but determined, not knowing where it would lead him, obedient only to the law of his inner calling. He believed himself led by Someone who leads us we know not where.

REFORMING HEARTS

Ignatius did not try to construct his own system as did many Renaissance figures. The Spiritual Exercises focus on personal reform, not the reform of Church doctrine or administration. He tried to purify the Church without overthrowing it, and preferred affirming and persuading to fighting or imposing. He expected personal experience and life to be more profitable than books or the world of ideas; the world's problems required a radical cure rather than mere knowledge. He cared less for scholarship than for the internal dispositions of those who would read the Bible and he cared about seeking out people to catechise along the roadsides and streets. He was an unsparing, sensitive companion-guide. He had his share of enemies, but he never let his heart be invaded by hatred toward those Christians, both false and official, who persecuted him. His basic impulse was not against anyone or anything. Rather, he had an obsession to help, to serve, to awaken and liberate people, not with beautiful theories or seductive schemes, but with the simple, down-to-earth question: 'What ought I to do?' The question he asked demanded decision and commitment.

'WHAT SHOULD I DO?'

During the year 1521–22, Ignatius was dreaming in Loyola while Luther was dreaming in Wartburg and Erasmus in Louvain. Each knew what it meant to be marginal, and each fostered a distinct type of rebellion. All three fought against the emptiness of the Christianity of their day. 'The only thing that remains Christian today is the name.' Ignatius said this, but it could also have been said by either Erasmus or Luther. All three felt deeply about the shambles into which the Church had fallen, but Ignatius reacted with neither criticism nor whimpering, and this he did out of a sense of decency and out of what he considered manliness. Decency, because one did not display the family's dirty laundry from the balcony, neither the dirty linen of his Loyola family nor his larger family, the Church; manliness, because a real man should not cry over dirty laundry, nor should he cast it aside; what he should do is clean it. In other words, Ignatius believed he should act to remedy the situation in the Church. He began by acting on himself; next, on those he came in contact with; and finally he acted in the temporal and geographical space that our activities can reach, a space always much larger than we think or can see. We are asked no more than to know how to stand face to face before each individual person or situation. The important thing is to work. While Ignatius worked in view of eternity, the limitations of history are inevitably present in what he did, as in all human effort.

MAN OF GOD

Ignatius had no time to speculate about issues that we might find important or diverting: he had enough to keep himself busy at each moment. He had questions regarding all types of emerging situations and events. He pondered about what to do when, having thought out the pros and cons, the Spirit did not yet speak with sufficient clarity. That same Spirit had once guided him through the capricious steps of a mule, through the will of a group, and through misadventures with Venetian ships. Initially, he had only the force of his unpolished word, which he did not proclaim harshly but whispered to each soul. He conquered for the good, through his quiet, contagious influence. 'One torch lights another.'

He did not seek anything for himself, but sought everything for his work, because the things we would never wish for ourselves we wish for those we love. Humbly, Ignatius continued along his way, without undue plans, pledges or methods – 'We have stumbled along.' By this time, he was followed by many who were 'ready for everything', even persecution. Six months after his death in 1556, a Cistercian monk made an inventory of the first attacks launched against the members of the Society. He stated: 'They say that they are introducing innovation; that they arrogantly attribute to themselves the name of Jesus; that they do not dress like friars; that they do not sing the canonical hours in choir. There are still others who criticise them because they are too much involved with the people, while others complain that they have grown too fast in a very short time.' Then, referring to Ignatius, he concluded: 'That little man of God had the patience to suffer all these things.'

This is a concise definition of what was coming to an end, the closing of 'the adventure of a poor Christian'. His pathway, one among many others, passed through Ethiopia, Brazil, Japan, Germany; made its inroads through the palace of the Duke of Gandia and the court of John III of Portugal, penetrated the lecture halls and porters' lodges of any number of colleges, and wended its way, too, through the kitchen of Santa Maria della Strada, Saint Mary of the Way, in Rome.

Ignatius believed he should act to remedy the situation in the Church.

What concrete step can you take to help 'to remedy the situation in the Church'?

70. Last Days, July 1556

BUSY TO THE END

By the beginning of 1556, Ignatius's health had shown considerable decline. He tried to disguise his suffering, but one who knew him said that it was a miracle that he was still alive. His gallstone attacks became more persistent, and to these were added low-grade fevers. He could no longer say Mass, his few hours of sleep were interrupted by an array of physical ailments and he took his meals in bed. He would spend a few hours working in the late afternoons of those days when the pain subsided, preoccupied by a whole raft of problems, among which were the apostasy of Ceylon, the Turkish menace, the Protestant world, some amendments to the Constitutions, problems in implementing the same Constitutions, economic crises, care of the sick, setting up the German Province, England's return to the Catholic Church, a College for Jerusalem, and so forth. He continued to dictate letters – some seven hundred during these last few months of his life – to Jesuits in various continents. His last letter was dated eight days before his death. Shortly after that date, he asked to see the doctor, who was in fact more worried about Laínez and some of the other sick Jesuits in the house in Rome. But from that moment, his health took an unexpected downward turn, and one can read in the letters that came out of Rome which announced the news of his death an unmistakable sense of surprise and shock, and even a certain hint of deception. The 'old saint', as he was referred to, left his brethren without their realising that he was going.

'I AM NEAR THE END'

Rome was under the sway of deadly, suffocating heat. To add to this torment, one medical man prescribed the customary remedy: all the windows in Ignatius's room were closed tight, and mountains of blankets were piled on top of him. Ignatius, who was a very gentle nurse while caring for the sick, was also a most obedient patient. Thus he perspired even more than ordinarily and was thereby further weakened. By the time another doctor changed this treatment, it was too late. At four o'clock on the afternoon of 30 July, Polanco responded to a call from Ignatius, who gave him an alarming mission: to go to Paul IV and tell him that he, Ignatius, 'was near the end and almost without hope of temporal life'. He asked for the pope's blessing for himself and also for Laínez. This, his last request, was an affirmation of Paul IV, who, in spite of his cold treatment and reserve toward Ignatius, represented for him the Church.

IN OTHERS' HANDS

For once, Ignatius was in a hurry, and he stressed his request with words that were frightening from a man who weighed every word: 'I am in such a bad way that the only thing I can do is die.' Unbelievably, the faithful Polanco did not take these words very seriously, thinking that Ignatius was exaggerating. Moreover, the mail courier was leaving for Spain that very day and Polanco had to get a large package of correspondence ready. He therefore told Ignatius that he would take care of the matter the next day, and he was not impressed by the strange insistence of the sick man: 'I would prefer today, rather than tomorrow, or at least as soon as possible. But do what you think best. I place myself entirely in your hands.' Polanco consulted with the doctor, was reassured that there was no reason to fear, and decided to put off fulfilling Ignatius's request until the next day. Thus Ignatius remained alone before death, silent and resigned. In 1550, he had told someone that the prospect of facing death had brought him immense joy and spiritual consolation. Now, as death really stood before him, he covered his feelings with silence. He simply put himself in the hands of God, the pope and the will of others. He renounced his own will and desires. During the night, the fifteen-year-old brother infirmarian whose bed was next to Ignatius's noticed that he was a bit agitated and that then he became quiet. One expression he repeated: 'Ay, Dios! Jesus.' (O, God! Jesus.) It was an expression of supplication, supreme surrender and hope.

AN ORDINARY DEATH

During the first visit after dawn, the community found Ignatius at the point of death. Polanco rushed off to accomplish his postponed mission and returned with the papal blessing, but Ignatius had died about seven o'clock. He died a death stripped of all its trappings. He died alone, without theatre, without the tears of companions at his bedside, without naming a vicar, without putting the definitive finish on the Constitutions, without bestowing blessings or final bits of advice, without transports or miracles, without sacraments, without the papal blessing, without having the final ritual prayers said for his soul. He died, as one witness noted with consternation, 'in the common way'. An autopsy was made on his corpse. Stones and more stones were found; these mute witnesses to his hidden suffering appeared in the liver, kidneys, lungs and even in one of the main arteries. Oh, and his feet! If the feet of Goethe were as delicate and beautiful as those of a maiden, Ignatius's feet were

Ignatius bequeathed a contagious enthusiasm and the certainty that God had guided him and had accomplished all.

covered with calluses hardened by so many European roads that took him 'to help people'. This was the pilgrim who had walked his way 'alone and on foot'.

A TREASURY OF HOPES

After four centuries, the autopsy on his soul is not yet finished. The death mask, the hastily made post-mortem portrait, the burial of his small corpse, the General Congregation and its problems, the future beatification and canonisation processes, the splendid altar in the Roman Church of the Gesu, Bernini's sculpture, the development of colleges and missions, the plans of Paul IV, and those of kings and princes, the magnificent basilica of Loyola, the praises and trials of the Society – all of these were for those whom Ignatius left behind. He bequeathed to them a contagious enthusiasm, a pattern of life, a treasury of hopes, the certainty that God had guided him and had accomplished all. In other words, he was leaving behind him the Society of Jesus.

By what would you like to be remembered?

Final sickness

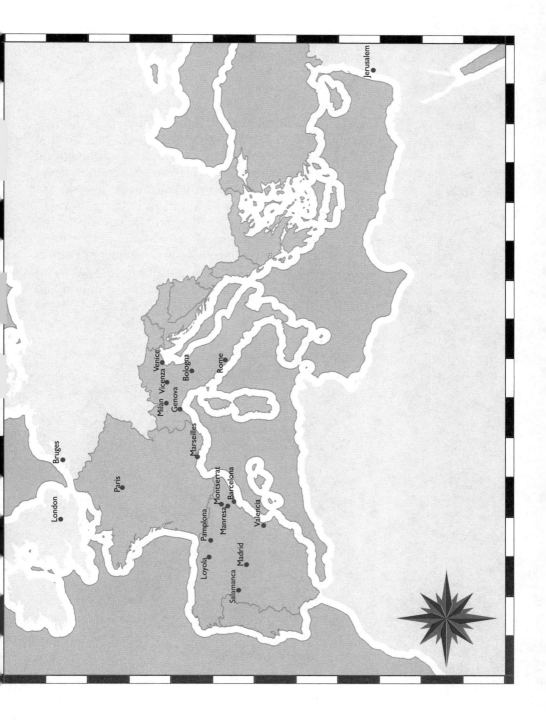